Eye on the Ball,
Mind on the Game

Eye on the Ball, Mind on the Game

An Easy Guide to Stress-Free Golf

Dr Arthur Jackson

Foreword by Laura Davies

SOUVENIR PRESS

First published in Australia and New Zealand
in 1995 by Bantam,
an imprint of Transworld Publishers (Aus) Pty Limited
and Transworld Publishers (NZ) Limited

First British Edition published 1997 by
Souvenir Press Ltd.,
43 Great Russell Street, London WC1B 3PA
and simultaneously in Canada

ISBN 0 285 63408 9

Printed in Great Britain by
WBC Book Manufacturers Limited,
Bridgend, Mid Glamorgan

Contents

Acknowledgments vii
Foreword ix
Introduction xi
Prologue: How to Use This Book xiv

1 Thinking Your Game of Golf 1
- Anxiety intrusion 2
- Adrenaline rush 3
- Concentration difficulties 5
- Mental camera lenses 7
- Using your subconscious 10

2 Confronting the Negative Game of Golf 13
- Confidence and self-belief 13
- How thoughts affect the game 16
- Negative self-talk 17

3 The Challenge Exercise 22
- Recognise, challenge and respond 22
- Scene 1: first tee jitters 25
- Scene 2: tricky approach shots 28
- Scene 3: intrusion of everyday life 31
- Using the challenge exercise 35

4	**Visualising the Positive Game of Golf**	**38**
	How professionals use visualisation	39
	How to use visualisation	43
5	**Improving Your General Approach**	**51**
	Pre-game anxiety	52
	Pre-game warm-up	54
	Sharpening visualisation skills	56
	Changing your concentration	60
	Coping with on-course tension	63
	Pacing yourself and your game	66
	How to enjoy a round of golf	69
6	**Problem Solving Course Guide**	**73**
	First tee anxiety	74
	Playing out of bunkers	80
	Fear of water hazards	82
	Putting to save shots	83
7	**Improving Your Scoring**	**88**
	Recovering your rhythm	89
	Coping with competition	92
	Developing a routine	97
	Final score	102
8	**Creative Relaxation**	**104**
	Playing in the 'Zone'	104
	Walking the mental plank	105
	Using Creative Relaxation	107
	Good golf	117
References		**118**
Index		**119**

Acknowledgments

It is difficult to write a book such as this without calling on the support of a great many people. Without their help, it would not be possible to make it all happen. I was very fortunate in being able to seek the advice and comments of a number of golf professionals. Obviously, these people are extremely skilled at the sport and have a wealth of experience which they were quite willing to share with me. In spite of busy playing and coaching schedules, tour professionals Jennifer Sevil and Ian Baker-Finch and Killara Golf Club professionals Dave Mercer and Greg Hohnen gave me a great deal of their time. They provided so many thoughtful and helpful comments on their experiences and were happy for me to incorporate these in the book. I owe each of them a special 'thank you' for their invaluable contributions.

I have appreciated, too, the help given me by the Australian Professional Golfers Association, Sirpa Hovi of the International Management Group and Don Johnson, Executive Director of the Australian Ladies Professional Golf Association. Each of these made life a great deal easier for me when I had need to contact particular individuals in their organisations.

No book can reach the light of day without the interest and encouragement of the publishing team. In this regard, I consider myself extremely lucky for I could not have had better and more enthusiastic support than I received from Transworld Publishers. In particular, I am indebted to two people: publisher Judith Curr without whose enthusiasm the book may well have faltered; and senior editor, Howard Gelman who was responsible for putting me back on track whenever I lost direction. I cannot express fully enough how much I have appreciated his wonderful help and gentle guidance throughout the book's preparation.

I want to take this opportunity, too, of expressing my deepest heartfelt thanks to my wife, Annie, who was a constant source of love, support and encouragement throughout. Not only did she give me helpful advice on the manuscript as it unfolded but also lifted my flagging spirits when necessary.

Finally, to all my golfing partners who, throughout the years have tolerated my golfing idiosyncrasies with good humour and who were also the source of much of the material for the book, may all your future rounds be successful ones.

Foreword

Someone once wrote that success in life often hinges on one seemingly small event or thing. In golf, for instance, a slight readjustment in your grip pressure during a round may be all that is necessary to take you to the top of the leader board. Nevertheless, I have learnt that having the correct technical skills and the right equipment is not always sufficient if you are to cope successfully with playing on the professional circuit. Most professional golfers now recognise that the other vital ingredient they need to work on is good control of the mind under the intense pressure of competition.

I was reminded of how easy it is to ignore or forget the importance of the mind factor during a recent tournament in Japan when Australian professional Jenny Sevil showed me a copy of the book *Eye on the Ball, Mind on the Game*. As I read through it, I became aware of how much I take for granted many of the psychological techniques so clearly set out by Dr Jackson. I recalled earlier days in my career when few if any of my fellow professionals thought of spending as much time training the mind as in refining their technical skills; it wasn't considered top priority in those days. But times have changed!

One thing I have learnt as a result of playing in the hard-knock school of the professional circuit is that controlling the mind in the heat of competition is far from being a 'seemingly small event'. It requires a lot of practice and diligence before it becomes second nature and, as with all golfing skills, needs a certain amount of professional guidance if you're to get the most out of it.

This is why I believe that *Eye on the Ball, Mind on the Game* will prove helpful to all golfers, irrespective of their talent. Dr Jackson has drawn upon his vast experience of helping sportspeople deal with competition pressure and has set out his techniques in such a way that they are not only easy to understand but can be applied to any golfer's game. One aspect of the book which caught my eye was the advice on dealing with negative self-talk, something that I'm sure troubles most golfers at some stage. The chapters on how to relax and how to use visualisation should also greatly benefit most people's game.

I am delighted to have the opportunity to write this foreword because although there is a wealth of books available on how to improve the technical aspects of your game, scant attention has been paid to coping with the psychological side. Here, at long last, is a book which will help you 'think well; play well without changing your swing'.

Good golfing.

Laura Davies
Member of the Women's Professional Golf European Tour and
US Ladies' Professional Golf Association

Introduction

One of the few challenges still remaining unconquered is the game of golf. After all, Everest has been scaled countless times and people have sailed single-handed around the world. The one area that seems to defy the efforts of players of all creed and colour is golf. Devout golfers desperately struggle to better their game but more often than not it proves to be an unequal battle.

What is it about golf that makes it so fascinating and also so desperately frustrating an experience that it is guaranteed to drive you to the edge of despair? It is difficult to pinpoint the exact reasons and it is probably a combination of factors. The principal one is the uncertainty of the game. No matter how well you may be playing, you can never be sure when this golden phase of your life will come to an abrupt end.

The second variable that makes golf so intriguing is the course itself. Unlike other sports, in golf you have to play on a constantly changing scene. It's unlikely your ball will finish on the same area of ground each time you play and your lie can vary from a relatively flat surface to one where it takes you all your time to maintain balance, and all this in the space of a few metres.

The third and most important variable is the mind element. I recall a sage old professional golfer telling me that golf is not so much a game of the hands but of the head. It took many years for this wise advice to sink in but there has never been a truer statement. Unfortunately, it's still the case that mind problems are perceived by many as being something of a stigma. You don't talk about them for fear of being thought strange. This is, perhaps, the major reason why so many golfers struggle each week to play consistently and close to their potential. They have failed to come to terms with the fact that golf is a game you play in your head and unless all is well in that area, you're destined to go on struggling.

In this book, I have set out a variety of techniques which are designed to help you deal with the anxiety which so often arises during a game. Controlling the mind is so vital because it functions like a computer or executive headquarters, directing everything within your game. Your swing, confidence, attitude and approach to the game all stem from the mind and unless all is well at that level, your game will suffer.

The aim of the book is to help you restructure your thinking and there are a number of techniques which will aid you in this. However, it would be nice if you could control your anxiety every day and, to this end, I have devoted a special chapter to show you how you can build relaxation exercises into your life. None of these techniques is meant as a 'quick-fix' but each is intended to provide you with long-term and persisting solutions. Admittedly, they call for a certain amount of time and effort on your part if they're to prove effective. This principle is true for most worthwhile things in life.

Your mind, then, lies at the centre of your game but because of its complexity, it's not easy to resolve tension or other problems through conscious willpower. This is the reason why you need help and direction. If this book does nothing else but make you more aware of the important role your mind plays in golf, it will have achieved a great deal.

Arthur Jackson
Sydney, Australia

Prologue: How to Use This Book

It's important that I clarify, right at the start, what I see as the role of the book. In doing this I've taken the licence of making certain assumptions. I assume that most serious golfers will have ensured the technical side of their game is satisfactory by taking lessons from a teaching professional. I cannot overemphasise the importance of professional instruction for it is the only way you can learn the fundamentals of the game, correct errors and bad habits, and develop a steady golf routine.

This book does not set out to solve basic problems with your swing or, in fact, deal with any of the mechanics or physical aspects of golf. Instead, its content is solely devoted to showing you how you can better apply your mind on the course so that you get much more out of your game.

My second assumption is that you want to improve and, to this end, I've outlined a series of exercises and routines which will help you achieve your goal. There are exercises dealing with breathing and pacing, and ones that offer specific techniques for visualisation. However, a word of caution should be sounded at the beginning: watch out for 'golf overload'. In other words, don't take too many 'exercises' with you to the golf course. The same principle applies to techniques taught you by your pro. Adopt a commonsense approach of working only on those things that are productive for you and make a point of practising them one at a time until each one becomes a routine part of your game.

It's an important rule in golf to 'keep it as simple as possible' or to use the acronym 'KISS' (keep it simple, stupid). This generally means that you should deal with one simple adjustment at a time, especially when you're playing in competition. Remember that golf is a game that can be played all your active life so you have lots of time to perfect your techniques and develop the correct mental approach. Take it easy, relax and work on one element at a time. The principle to keep in mind is that the game should always fascinate, challenge and enrich your life.

CHAPTER ONE

Thinking Your Game Of Golf

Golf was once described by Sir Winston Churchill, that well-known politician and writer of bygone years, as 'an ineffectual attempt to direct an uncontrollable sphere into an inaccessible hole with instruments ill-adapted to that purpose'. As an ardent golfing enthusiast, you would probably perceive these comments as being no more than the cynical and biased delusions of a non-golfer, someone who has never experienced the sheer thrill that arises from hitting a long, straight drive or sinking a seemingly impossible putt.

But this perception of golf is not nearly as unreasonable as it first appears. Few golfers are able to play to their potential on a consistent basis and it is this inconsistency that generally provokes the greatest frustration. The issue that troubles most golfers is why the game can be a joy one moment and a miserable and disturbing experience the next. There simply has to be an explanation for this sudden and inexplicable turn of fortune that can occur in as short a time as it takes to play a few holes.

Have you ever wondered why, for example, your swing can change in an instant from being a relaxed, rhythmical practice swing to one in which you lash at the ball more in hope than with any expectation of success? Gone is the full shoulder turn and cocking of the wrists followed by a smooth downswing and complete follow-through. Instead, you find yourself afflicted by a lightning-fast and incomplete backswing, and a downswing that proves to be no more than a wild lash at a perfectly still ball, associated with a series of movements reminiscent of a dervish dance. It's as though your mind has become fixated with the idea of hitting the ball as quickly as possible for fear that something unforeseen may happen to it.

Anxiety intrusion

The answer isn't too difficult to find. The change in your swing pattern is not because of some fault in your physical makeup but rather, in what your mind is doing to you. You were able, in this example, to swing easily in practice because you were relaxed. Nothing important hinged on whether your practice swing was perfect or not, and so your grip and swing were free from the inhibiting effects which anxiety creates in your body.

However, the moment you are confronted by the ball in play, the whole situation changes. Self-doubt and negative thinking start to intrude and your thoughts become dominated by the 'what-ifs' of golf. A few examples will give you the flavour of what I mean:

- What if I slice this drive out-of-bounds; wouldn't that be a terrible way to start a round

- What if I hit this shot into the water like I did the last time I played? I'd feel awful about losing another ball.
- What if I hit my ball into that bunker? I'm hopeless at playing out of it.

These anxious and negative thoughts are powerful in nature and set in train a whole series of unwanted effects in the body. Suddenly you're aware of how the feel of the hands on the grip seems to have changed. The relaxed, comfortable feel of the hands working as one is replaced by an increased sense of tightening. This tension is soon transmitted to the arms, shoulders and back and the formerly fluid takeaway and backswing are transformed into a restricted and rapid series of movements.

At this point any hope of producing a sound swing is more a question of luck than design. You start the downswing far too early and your problems become compounded by your eagerness to see what has happened to your shot. This premature 'look-up' may only be a matter of milliseconds in duration but it's sufficient to interfere with the critical point of impact between clubhead and ball. Inevitably, the fate of your shot becomes a lottery and the ball can fly off the clubface on a range of trajectories varying from almost ground level to one that would be a danger to low-flying aircraft.

Adrenaline rush

You may have become aware of these instantaneous changes in your swing pattern and endeavoured to correct the situation by trying to relax or trying to keep your head still. Have you noticed how singularly unsuccessful these conscious efforts have been in alleviating the problems? There is a good reason for this and it's all to do with your internal chemistry.

Whenever you become anxious, whether on the golf course or anywhere else, your body responds by releasing into the blood stream increased amounts of a hormone called adrenaline. This chemical is important to your well-being and safety in life because it's a vital part of your fight-or-flight mechanism. Adrenaline mobilises your blood sugar reserves, increases your alertness and concentration and enables you to move quickly or defend yourself if you are under any sort of threat.

When you become anxious, your body perceives even everyday events as threatening and this stimulates the release of huge amounts of adrenaline. One of the major spin-offs, and one that you don't really need in golf, is that it leads to increased muscle tension. Your muscles become super-aroused and ready to react to any call for action. However, in this state they are also excessively tense and tight and it's this increased muscle tone that accounts for the change in your swing pattern. Once this process has started, no amount of conscious effort on your part will reverse the negative effects. Instead, as you will learn later, you need to develop ways of subconscious mind control to counteract this problem.

The adrenaline surge also has the effect of speeding up the reactions of the body and particularly muscle movements. This accounts for your swing becoming so much faster when you are nervous and applies as much to putting as to hitting a driver or iron. The only way you can effectively and consistently counteract this tendency to quicken your backswing is by getting rid of the anxiety, and this is where relaxation techniques will help.

Concentration difficulties

We all know that the ability to concentrate at specified times is essential if you want to perform to your maximum. It is even more crucial in sport and it's something that many sports people find hard to maintain for any extended time. Unfortunately, concentration is easily fragmented, especially when you are anxious. The anxious mind is already overloaded with negative and intrusive thoughts and it finds it difficult to maintain the necessary focus on the needs of the moment.

This overload situation is more likely to happen to you if you are already under pressure at work or have personal or family problems. It would be unreasonable to expect that you can switch off from these difficulties just because you have laced on your golf shoes and taken yourself out onto the course. Yet many golfers do harbour these unrealistic expectations. As you may have found, these mental pressures make concentration even more difficult. Instead of focusing on the game, you find your mind wandering on to other, non-golf related matters and this can happen at critical times, such as when putting or playing an approach shot. When this occurs, it will certainly work against your game and instead of your golf round providing a break away from life's pressures, it will only add to your frustration and stress.

Although concentration can sometimes prove difficult to maintain in any sport, it is especially so in golf. The most obvious reason for this is that it takes a long time to play a round. You just have too much time to think. Consider how long it takes to walk to your ball or how much time your pre-shot routine takes and you can see why there is ample opportunity for anxious thoughts to take hold. These negative thoughts act as a catalyst for a variety of anxiety problems, the principal one being loss of concentration.

Most golfers unfamiliar with the correct psychological approach tend to try to correct their concentration difficulties by falling back on familiar remedies such as resorting to conscious effort or willpower. This would appear to be a logical thing to do but although you may find it helpful for a short period, it's destined to fail in the long-term because the problems really lie outside conscious control.

You will understand the rationale behind this more clearly if I give you an uncomplicated and familiar view of how the mind functions. It's helpful to think of your mind as operating on two separate levels. The one of which you are most aware is the conscious mind and the second is the subconscious. Naturally, there is a great deal of interchange of thoughts between the two but without doubt the most powerful control over your life is exerted by your subconscious mind. This is the 'storeroom' or 'data base' for all life's experiences. It is the executive headquarters that controls everything that happens both within your body and in the emotional aspects of your life.

It is also the centre from which many of your anxieties arise and this is why any conscious attempt to control problems such as poor concentration is relatively ineffective. What you need is a way of being able to access your subconscious level so that you can 'reprogram' yourself. Your aim is to get your mind to function in a way that will benefit rather than undermine your game.

Mental camera lenses

Good concentration is important if you want to play consistent golf. It is a game that requires you to be able to maintain a focus of attention for long periods and this can be tiring and difficult unless performed correctly. Unlike many other sports such as tennis or cricket, golf is not a reflex game. The ball is perfectly still and requires no sudden reflex movements to make contact with it. Instead, you have an excess of time available to address the ball and hit your shot. It's this situation that can disturb your concentration.

A useful method that will improve your ability to concentrate is to differentiate between the two types of focus you need while playing:

First, there is the intense concentration you call on when you are going through your set-up routine. This involves focusing on your grip, the ball position, alignment and your stance. This type of concentration can be tiring if you try to maintain it for any length of time and should be restricted to a few minutes at the most.

The second form of concentration involves opening-up your focus so that you take in a wider view of the course. You will want to consider such things as wind direction, the position of hazards such as water and bunkers, the slope of the fairway and pin position on the green. The challenge to maintaining an effective concentration is being able to switch smoothly from one focus to the other as the situation demands.

Some golfers, such as Lee Trevino, are able to switch easily from the intense, narrow-focused attention needed when hitting the ball to a more relaxed easy-going approach as they walk to their next shot. This should be your aim too, but it's not something that comes easily unless you have a technique to call on.

Let me give you one that is not only easy to remember but quickly trains your mind to change focus in an automatic and unconscious way. Think of the two fields of concentration necessary for good golf as being similar to the lenses of a camera. The narrow focus you need to draw on when setting up for a shot is like a close-up lens and the broader view of the golf scene is like a wide-angle lens.

As you go through your set-up routine, consciously feel that you're narrowing your attention, bringing your close-up lens into operation. The aim is to have total involvement in all aspects of the set-up and, if you are doing this successfully, you will find that you are no longer distracted by intrusive thoughts or things and people around you. This is important, for so many golfers are overly aware of what is happening around them or are bothered by such things as a significant breeze. Whenever this happens, it's an indication that you are not fully focusing with your close-up lens and this will probably have a significant impact on how well you hit the ball.

Once you have played your shot, it's time to switch to your wide-angle lens. You have ample opportunity to do this as you walk to your ball. Why not use the time constructively to assess the slope of the fairway, any hazards you may have to negotiate on the way to the green, the direction of any wind and the type of shot you want to play?

This process has the added advantage of breaking the cycle of intense concentration required whenever you use your close-up mental lens. Then, when you are ready to play your next shot, remind yourself to switch back to your close-up perspective of grip, ball position and alignment. As you go through your round, you 'switch focus' from a close-up lens to a wide-angle one as the situation demands and as if you were a walking camera.

It's probably fair to say that most golfers use this type of technique without being aware they are doing so. The reason I suggest you think of the concentration process as being similar to using two camera lenses is that it reminds you to change your focus of attention on a consistent basis. It's easy to get trapped in one or other focus and not realise it's happening to you.

A good example of this, and one which most golfers can relate to, is when you are still dwelling on a previous poor shot or a 'bad hole' even as you are going through your next pre-shot routine. This typifies the way the mind can become easily distracted by negative thinking, especially when you become anxious.

You can also disturb your concentration during set-up by constantly moving your focus, one moment looking at your grip and ball position, and the next the fairway or green. The main disadvantage of doing this is that it breaks up the intense, narrow focus you need before hitting the ball. A trick that will help you keep your close-up lens in constant use is to select a leaf or tuft of grass half to one metre in front of the ball and which is on the line along which you want to aim. This object then becomes part of your narrowed field of focus and, with a little practice, you will soon learn to put your wide-angled lens to one side as you are setting up the shot to be played.

Using your subconscious

I'm sure you can recall some life situation where you have made a conscious decision to react in a particular way but some 'inner voice', sometimes called intuition or a sixth sense, tells you that even though it appears a logical solution, it's not the correct path to follow. Have you ever evaluated what happened when you decided to stick to your original decision? The chances are that the results were not nearly as successful as you would have wished.

That 'inner voice' you heard could be likened to your subconscious mind talking to you. Your decision to ignore it was probably not a wise choice. Generally, the subconscious denotes your true feelings. Your conscious mind, on the other hand, can be logical but perhaps not emotionally accurate. Obviously, conscious decisions have successful outcomes but sometimes they can be hopelessly wrong.

The subconscious mind is the storeroom for all your past experiences and learned behaviours. It has a vast reservoir of knowledge and experience to draw on whenever you ask it to guide you. This is certainly the situation with golf. If you think of how many balls you've hit with each club in the past, it would be reasonable to expect that the repetition factor alone should improve your game. For the majority of golfers, though, this is not the case and no matter how hard they strive to improve, progress always appears frustratingly slow.

If you fall into this category and took the time to analyse why this happens, you would find that in many instances your game deteriorated when you lost trust in your subconscious mind. Even though you may have worked diligently to 'groove' a sound swing, under the pressure of competition all those well-learned muscle movements are lost because you have chosen to override them with conscious effort. Whenever you start to think about various aspects of your swing or make spontaneous changes to your grip during a round, you are counteracting all those well-rehearsed actions. Unfortunately, these conscious changes act against your game.

So where does the answer lie? Let's review the process: First, you establish a good swing pattern and, for most people, this can only be achieved through professional coaching. The other vital ingredient for a sound swing is practice, practice and more practice. This is the way correct muscle movements, initiated by professional coaching, become automatic and unconscious responses. Then, and most importantly, you have to learn to put complete trust in your subconscious. However, the one element which will cause you to lose faith in your 'inner voice' will be anxiety. The moment anxiety enters the picture, it seems to act as a catalyst for conscious effort and willpower to take over. Instead of a smooth, relaxed swing, you suddenly start trying to hit the ball harder with the unwanted result that your routine becomes disrupted.

One way you can overcome this tendency is to make a commitment to yourself that no matter what happens, you will resist the temptation to make any radical changes to your game during a competition round. If any drastic changes need to be made, they are better done in practice. Remember, though, that this decision is not nearly as easy to follow as it first appears.

Anxiety seems to have the effect of making you want to tamper with your swing or grip, and dealing with this really comes back to taking the appropriate steps to reduce the anxiety factor.

CHAPTER TWO

Confronting the Negative Game of Golf

There is little doubt that anxiety will create a whole series of negative effects on your game. One area that is usually the first affected is your self-confidence.

Confidence and self-belief

Everyone is familiar with the important part self-confidence plays in life. If you believe in yourself and what you're doing, there is a greater chance of success no matter what the challenge. This is never more true than in golf, when being confident about your skill is undoubtedly the essential factor in hitting the ball well.

Unfortunately self-confidence is fragile and it takes very little to undermine it. Amazing as it may seem, even something as simple as hitting one poor shot or playing one hole badly can sometimes be enough to dent it and produce a carry-over effect on the rest of your game.

What usually causes this sudden change in confidence is, once again, the intrusion of anxiety coupled with negative self-talk. I use the term **negative self-talk** to refer to that inner conversation we have with ourselves. It consists of critical, often demoralising thoughts that have a profound effect on our playing ability. Most golfers can recall occasions when they have been playing with ease and then, quite suddenly, they hit a poor shot. Immediately, they start to think:

- What a terrible shot.
- I don't know why that happened.
- Wouldn't it be awful if I went on hitting the ball like that?
- I hope it doesn't happen again.

Once this negative self-talk takes hold, it's quickly followed by anxious feelings and you start to tighten. As I mentioned earlier, this increased tension will adversely affect your grip pressure, restrict your shoulder turn and abbreviate your follow-through. Most of all, though, your mind becomes overloaded with self-doubt and the result is an undermining of your confidence. This usually has the effect of causing ill-timed movements that will complicate your swing problems. So you can see from this example how easy it is for negative thoughts to lead to a complete loss of confidence in your game.

It's also common to develop the habit of undermining your own self-confidence by 'programming' negative thoughts into your mind whenever you are confronted with playing certain shots. This tends to happen when you've encountered the same problems in the past, such as with approach shots to the green that require finesse and a sense of 'touch'. That delicate pitch you need to float over the bunker so that it nestles close to the pin suddenly becomes a frightening prospect.

When this happens, self-doubt and negative self-talk dominate your thinking and it quickly triggers feelings of anxiety about the outcome of the shot. Your mind is locked in on anxious thoughts:

- I hope I can hit this shot correctly.
- Wouldn't it be terrible if I put it into the bunker just as I did the last time?
- It took me three strokes to get out.

What you must remember is that your mind will soon transform this negative thinking into negative responses. Your swing becomes far too quick, your head moves long before it should, and the ball is either projected across the green off the club's leading edge at the speed of a Formula One racing car or else drops a sickening metre or so in front of you.

The most important effect that arises from losing confidence is that your rhythm becomes disrupted. Good rhythm and tempo are essential for a sound swing but they are usually the first elements affected by anxiety and loss of confidence. The fluid components of a relaxed swing are replaced by what feels like a series of cogwheel movements and the harder you consciously strive to re-establish your rhythm, the more fragmented it becomes. This is just another of the many frustrations created by your anxious mind.

How thoughts affect the game

Your inner conversation or self-talk can sometimes have profound effects on the way you hit a shot. Most people are acquainted with a method used to alleviate this loss of confidence that is known as 'positive thinking'. It has been explained in a variety of ways as a necessary stepladder to success.

But, have you ever noticed that whenever you feel anxious or nervous about some aspect of your golf, no matter how much positive thinking you try to instil into yourself, it has little or no effect on easing your concerns? This is because the negative thinking associated with anxiety tends to dominate and screen out positive thoughts, rendering them ineffective.

Another drawback of relying solely on positive thinking is that it usually leads to you consciously trying harder to rectify the problems of the moment. This, in turn, causes you to become even more tense so that your grip pressure tightens, the swing quickens and you lose tempo.

I'm not suggesting that you abandon all positive thinking. This would be unrealistic and unnecessary. However, it's important that you learn alternative ways of dealing with negative self-talk and incorporate these into positive thinking.

If you are a person who relies heavily on positive thinking to improve your performance, make sure that the goals you set for yourself are realistic and achievable. Most professional golfers and low handicap amateurs bring a great deal of positive thinking into their game. Australian tour professional Jenny Sevil typifies this approach: 'Even if I bogey a hole, I tell myself I can birdie the next few . . . Positive chatter is a constant feature of my game'.

Few handicap golfers would dare give themselves this sort of positive reinforcement simply because they lack the expertise to make it happen. The answer lies in avoiding the use of thoughts that are likely to prove difficult or impossible to achieve. If the 'positive thinking' fails to materialise, it creates a sense of failure and causes you to become even more dispirited with your game.

Negative self-talk

One of the inescapable facts of life is that we are all sensitive to things others say to us and we react accordingly. Our response to other people's remarks is more marked if they come from those we love, fear or whom we perceive to be in a position of authority and this accounts for the effectiveness of subtle gamesmanship.

In the same way, your mind is extremely responsive to thoughts that you generate within yourself. This inner conversation or self-talk is a constant feature of life and usually takes place outside your conscious awareness. This is also why it is so dangerous at times. It can happen when you least expect it and the result is that you feel nervous and anxious.

Negative self-talk is also the foundation on which self-doubts are built and it's a short step from there to losing confidence and finding it hard to cope. This is why learning how to deal with negative self-talk is such an important issue if you are to improve your mental approach to golf.

Identifying negative self-talk

What are the elements of negative self-talk and how can you identify it? The principal feature of this type of thinking is when your concerns about what may go wrong with a particular shot are based on beliefs that are illogical and irrational. In other words, they are not based on fact, but rather on what you fear may happen. They are illogical because, although you are unable to substantiate them, you are still plagued by a deeply held belief that something terrible is going to happen to your shot. You expect the very worst outcome when you hit the ball even though you have little evidence or proof to justify your fear.

Negative self-talk can be recognised by certain phrases or words such as:

- what if
- I hope that
- awful
- terrible
- If only

These usually preface a series of ongoing negative thoughts. Let me give you three golfing situations where negative thinking commonly arises:

1. **You are on the first tee and become aware of other golfers watching you address the ball. Without warning, your mind is suddenly besieged by a rush of negative thoughts: 'I hope my swing is all right. Wouldn't it be awful if I muck-up this shot. I'd feel so embarrassed in front of all these people. What if I hit it out of bounds? That would be a terrible way to start the round'.**

2. **You're confronted with playing a tee shot over a water**

hazard: 'I always seem to have difficulty with this hole. What if I hit the ball into the water like I did last time? I'd better use an old ball in case I do. That fairway seems a really long way off this tee today'.

3. You're faced with having to play an approach shot to the green over a bunker: 'I must stay down on this shot. Wouldn't it be awful if I land in the bunker? It's so deep and I'm not all that good at playing bunker shots. I hope I can get it out first time'.

These three examples of negative self-talk are typical of what can trouble golfers during a round. Unfortunately, the entire sequence has a profound effect on the way you play your shot. Instead of hitting your drive sweetly down the centre of the fairway in the first example, you are more inclined to produce a vicious hook or slice. And in the other two examples, your ball will certainly finish in the water hazard or bunker.

Because your mind is controlling everything that happens in your body, it follows that if you think negatively then you will react negatively. This mechanism is so powerful that once any form of negative self-talk starts to intrude on your game it will rapidly create a sense of increased tension, grip pressure will tighten and your swing will become restricted and abnormal. Added to this, you'll find it almost impossible to 'stay down' when you hit because of your desire to see whether your worst fears have been realised.

If you are troubled by negative self-talk, you may get some solace from learning that you are not alone, for even tour hardened elite golfers sometimes succumb to it. Jenny Sevil who has many years experience on both the Australian and Japanese tour circuit, admits that early in her professional career negative self-talk often intruded into her game: 'If I bogied the first hole, for example, I would think "well, here we go again. I'm off to a rotten start". I found these negative thoughts usually had a negative effect on the rest of my game'.

Overcoming negative self-talk

Even though negative self-talk is such a common foe on the golf course, as it is in life, few people seem to have any effective ways of dealing with it. The approach for most people is to try not to think of the thing that is bothering them. But, this technique is doomed to failure because the more you try to shut out particular thoughts, the more they will trouble you.

You are really conditioning your mind to focus on them even more intently with the result that they will preoccupy your whole thinking process. If, for instance, you tell yourself you are not going to move your head when you hit the ball, the last thought before you swing is associated with head movement and this almost guarantees that it will happen.

In case you need convincing that your mind reacts to your most immediate thought, let me give you a simple test:

> For the next few moments, try not to think of the colour 'blue'. You will probably notice that, even though you had no reason to think of 'blue' before I suggested it, suddenly there is an increased awareness of things associated with that colour. You may be surprised, for example, by how much blue is in the room around you or in the clothing you're wearing.

The point of this exercise is to demonstrate how easy it is for your mind to become totally focused on the last thought you had and in golf that's usually the thing causing you the most concern at that moment. Combating negative self-talk is one of the fundamental elements in regaining confidence and stability on the golf course.

CHAPTER THREE

The Challenge Exercise

In the previous chapter we discussed negative self-talk: how it starts and its debilitating effects on our playing ability. Fortunately, there is an effective way of counteracting negative self-talk. Psychologists call this technique 'cognitive restructuring'. Before you become frightened off by this jargon, let me reassure you that it's not nearly as complex as it sounds.

Recognise, challenge and respond

For our purposes, we will call this technique the **challenge exercise** and it's a simple three-step process:

1. **recognise** negative self-talk
2. **challenge** your negativity
3. **respond** with positive thinking

The technique centres on the need to prove to yourself that the thoughts which are creating your fears have no logical foundation to them. If, for example, you're concerned about chipping over the bunker, you can be sure that the last thought preoccupying your mind is the bunker and what might go wrong if you land in it. However, there is no logical reason for believing you are definitely going to hit it there. You can't prove to yourself beyond question that it's going to occur. Instead, your thoughts are being fuelled by your concerns of what might happen. As you have already seen, it is not enough to tell yourself you won't think of the bunker. This will only intensify your awareness of it.

Recognise negative self-talk

As noted, dealing with negative thoughts is a three-step process. First, you must recognise they exist. I have already suggested that you recognise the negativity of such phrases as:

- I hope that
- Wouldn't it be awful
- If only

Certain other words can also place pressure on you to perform and these include 'must' ('I must get this putt otherwise I'll bogey the hole') and 'should' ('I should have used a different club . . . now I'm in real trouble').

Challenge your negativity

The second step is to challenge these negative thoughts. Here, you want to prove unequivocally to yourself that your thinking is ridiculous and illogical. The simplest way you can do this is to ask yourself either of these questions.
What evidence do I have:

- What evidence do I have that I'm definitely going to mess-up this shot?

What absolute proof do I have:

- What absolute proof do I have that I'm going to hit this shot into the bunker?

Silently posing either of these questions to yourself allows you the opportunity of debating each answer until you reach a point where you are convinced there is no logic to your fears.

Respond with positive thinking

The third part of the sequence centres on your need to respond to the problem by replacing negative thinking with positive, logical and realistic thoughts or affirmations. Now, positive thinking will be effective because you have nullified the more powerful negative thoughts. Your mind is then in a better position to 'believe' and accept the positive affirmations.

The best way to demonstrate how the process of recognise–challenge–respond works is to present three common golfing situations where negative self-talk invariably prospers. Some of the expressions I use may not be identical to yours but I'm sure they will give you an idea of how to apply the technique.

Scene 1: first tee jitters

You are waiting to hit off the first tee and it is a match play event. Your opponent has hit a particularly good drive down the fairway and after a loosening practice swing you settle over your ball. Suddenly, you become excessively aware that many people, including the club professional, are watching every move you make.

There is an imperceptible increase in tension in the shoulders and neck and your hands feel tighter on the grip. Without warning, a series of thoughts flashes through your mind and as disturbing as they are to your concentration, it seems as though you can do nothing to stop them. The process of negative self-talk has already started to take hold of your game.

Recognise negative self-talk

- He's hit a great shot.
- I hope I can match it.
- Wouldn't it be awful if I mess it up?
- What if I hit it out of bounds or into those trees on the left?
- That would be so embarrassing with all these people watching.
- I don't feel comfortable with my stance.
- I must try to hit this shot easily.

- I hope I don't slice it like I did the last time.
- I'd better play away from trouble and grip the club a bit firmer with my right hand.
- I must stay down on this shot and make sure I don't sway on the backswing.

Challenge your negativity

Once you know what type of negative self-talk is affecting you, you must deal with it. There is only one effective way of doing this and that is to issue a challenge to your negative thinking. The aim is to prove to yourself beyond any shadow of doubt that it's quite illogical.

Even though your mind is being inundated with negative thoughts, it's quite difficult under the pressures of the moment to know what to do with them. The solution lies in asking yourself a demand question, one that you must answer. It must be phrased in such a way that you can't sidestep it by giving yourself a vague response.

There are two questions you'll find helpful to start the challenge:

- What proof do I have that I'm going to hit the ball out of bounds?
- What evidence do I have that I am going make a mess of this shot just because everyone's watching me?

Often the mind will try to be devious and rather than giving yourself a logical reply, the thought might pass through your mind that you've done it before, the inference being that this justifies it happening again.

You are then faced with a second challenge:

- But just because I've hit it out of bounds in the past, does this mean that I'm definitely going to do it this time?

Depending upon how anxious and jittery you feel at that moment, your mind may continue to be difficult and strike back with yet another negative thought, such as:

- I guess there's a chance I could do so.
- After all, nothing is certain in this world.

At this stage, you really need to take control and break the sequence of negative thinking. It's often helpful to use humour or a ridiculous question as a final means of demonstrating to yourself how stupid and illogical are your concerns:

- On that basis, if I had a headache last time I played golf, does that mean I'm going to have a headache every time I play?

Obviously, if you've worked hard on your swing and your game, you will always have the ability to hit a good shot. There is no justification for thinking that poor play is inevitable because of your state of mind. By using this simple internal dialogue, you can prove unequivocally to yourself that your concerns about what could go wrong with your shot are completely irrational and unfounded.

Respond with positive thinking

Now that you've proved there is no logical basis for thinking in negative terms, you move on to the third and final stage of dealing with this unwanted thought process. Once you have nullified negative self-talk, you can instil positive thoughts or affirmations.

Before the challenge step, positive thinking has little or no impact because it tends to be overwhelmed by the more powerful effects of anxious, negative thoughts. But now that your mind is free of these constraints, it's able to absorb and respond to the positive thoughts:

- There's no reason why I can't swing easily.
- I'll lighten my grip a little and make sure I get a full shoulder turn (here you're bringing in one key swing thought).
- I feel so much more comfortable.
- If the ball doesn't go precisely where I want, it's not the end of the world.
- I can feel the weight of the clubhead in my practice waggle.
- I'll just swing smoothly and let the club do the work.

Scene 2: tricky approach shots

Most handicap golfers experience a sense of nervousness before attempting to hit a delicate pitch over a cavernous bunker. The predominant thought becomes the bunker and all the problems that could arise if you have to play out of it. By now we can see a familiar pattern resulting from negative self-talk.

Recognise negative self-talk

- I must get this shot close to the hole.
- If only that pin wasn't tucked in so close to the bunker.
- I hope I don't muck it up.
- It'll cost me a shot and I hate having to play out of this bunker.
- I always seem to make a mess of it.
- If only I'd hit my previous shot better, I wouldn't be in this position now.

If your mind becomes assailed by these type of thoughts, you'll probably make a quick, anxious swing at the ball. It's not too difficult to imagine the outcome. The chances are that you'll finish in the dreaded bunker or propel the ball across the green at lightning speed. Either way, you're faced with a recovery shot and, as hard as it may be to accept, all this can be attributed to negative self-talk.

Challenge your negativity

- OK. So I have to play my next shot over that bunker.
- Is there any reason why I can't do this?
- After all, I have several clubs in my bag designed for the purpose.

Your perverse subconscious may prove to be a little difficult this particular day and raise counter-arguments that something could go wrong with the shot:

- But what if I hit it badly?
- I'm not too good at playing these short shots around the green.
- I never seem to know how much backswing to take.
- I hope I don't leave it short.
- This bunker is so hard to get out of.

In this type of situation, it is worthwhile drawing on a little humour as a counter-attack mechanism:

- What's the worst thing that will happen to me if I hit it into the bunker?
- Will everyone laugh at me?
- Will they refuse to play with me if I do?

Questions such as these are sufficient to change your whole approach from fear to confidence.

Respond with positive thinking

- I've played this type of shot a thousand times and nothing disastrous happened even if I didn't always play it as well as I should have done.

- I'll follow the technique suggested by my pro and let my hands feel easy and light on the grip.
- I'll keep my weight well forward throughout the swing.
- I'll hit down into the ball and let the club do the work.
- I've plenty of time to see how it's all worked out after I've played the shot.
- No need to rush anything.
- I know I can play this shot well.

Once you have gone through this brief thought ritual, you must place complete trust in your subconscious mind. If you allow your mental computer to take control over your shot, you'll find it rarely lets you down.

Scene 3: intrusion of everyday life

If you are under pressure at work, have problems at home, or lead a busy life in general, you have probably noticed how difficult it is to switch off from these concerns when you go out to play golf. Your mind is so overloaded with worry about personal issues that it finds it hard to shut out these anxieties and focus on your game.

Recognise negative self-talk

Sometimes fitting in a game of golf may also mean that you have to make a hurried trip to the course immediately after a busy day at work or home. It is not surprising, therefore, that when you are preoccupied with other problems, your game is likely to be disturbed by a constant flow of distracting, negative thoughts, such as:

- I just can't keep my mind on my game today.
- Perhaps I shouldn't be out here.
- I feel badly about leaving my partner to cope while I'm away.
- I forgot to arrange that appointment next week.
- I just can't relax.
- I'm hitting the ball badly and I was so looking forward to this game.
- I'm not really enjoying this very much.
- I'd been better off staying home.

This type of self-talk is common enough nowadays and shows that anxiety is a pernicious and constant problem no matter where you are or what you're doing. What you need to realise is that once anxiety takes hold, it is present 24 hours a day until you do something active to deal with it. Learning relaxation techniques helps you and I will talk more about these later in the book. However, your immediate goal is to deal with the flow of negative self-talk which is interfering with your game and leisure time.

Challenge your negativity

Because of the variety of complex thoughts rushing through your mind, most of which have nothing to do with golf, you need to develop a readily available strategy for counteracting these. Unless you do this, golf is going to prove more of a stressor to you than a form of relaxation and time-out from your worries. Here is a typical challenge situation:

- I realise I've all sorts of problems in the office but do I have any reason to believe that if I go on worrying about them out here on the course, it will resolve one single thing?

Your mind can, on occasions, be extremely devious by providing an apparently logical response:

- But I just don't seem able to stop worrying about things even though I know it's stupid to do so.

In everyday life, you've probably heard many people say that they can't stop themselves worrying. To some extent their comment is not without justification, for worry and anxiety go together. In allowing themselves this kind of response, they are admitting they have absolutely no control over their thoughts. However, the situation will only improve if they lessen their anxiousness.

You, too, can change how you think. It sometimes takes a little effort to make those changes but it's time well spent. Again, it's useful to fall back and give yourself a ridiculous counter-argument:

- If I worry is it going to help my problems or if I believe I can't stop worrying, why don't I set aside a special time for worry straight after the game?

- I'll stay in the locker room and just sit and worry.
- I'll do nothing else but worry, worry, worry.
- The more I worry, the better I'll get.

This technique may seem a bit of an oversimplification but it does work by proving to yourself that it's useless to worry about things whether on the golf course or anywhere else. Worry always intensifies your anxiety and it resolves nothing.

Respond with positive thinking

- No, that's stupid.
- Even if I gave myself special worry-time it wouldn't make any difference.
- It would make more sense to really focus on my golf so that I can enjoy it.
- It'll make me feel much more relaxed.
- I can take a fresh look at things tomorrow when I have to deal with my problems.
- But just for now, I'll focus on each shot with the same intensity as I did on my worries.

Here, you are concentrating on your game and not on your problems. You have replaced your worrying thoughts with positive ones. While all of us must deal with life's problems at some time, hopefully, we won't do it on the golf course.

Using the challenge exercise

If you feel you will never have enough time during an actual game to go through this challenge exercise without incurring the wrath of the match committee and your fellow golfers for holding up play, please be reassured. Although it may appear to be a lengthy procedure, it takes very little time to recognise and defeat your negative self-talk. To speed-up the process, you will find it helpful to learn a few stock phrases so that you can use these at the appropriate time. Here are examples of useful challenge questions:

- What's the worst thing that could happen to me if I hit this shot poorly?
- Would it be the end of the world if I don't sink this putt?
- Just because I've played a bad shot, does that mean the rest of my round is ruined?
- What proof do I have that I can't sink this metre-long putt?
- Is there some unknown force which is going to make me slice this shot into the trees?
- Do I have any evidence that I can't ever play this pitch shot correctly?
- Just because I played this shot badly before, does that mean I must do it the same way again?

The benefit of these readily available questions is that they provide an immediate counter-attack to negative self-talk and with practice, you can change your thinking from negative to positive in a matter of moments.

It may seem hard to believe that we can indulge in so much inner dialogue and yet it is fairly typical of the thoughts that trouble many golfers when they are going through their set-up routine. Apart from the obvious negativity, our inner thought process indicates how easily the mind can become burdened with distractions and, usually, we don't realise it's happening. Jack Nicklaus has good advice regarding how many key thoughts to allow yourself during your set-up:

> 'On average, I'd say that two is about the handicap golfer's limit, and that he'd be better off most of the time with only one key swing thought'.

The usual result from a constant flow of negative thoughts is that you develop negative feelings about what is going to happen to your swing. You believe that your shot will be unsuccessful, which only serves to undermine your self-confidence. Finally, the combination of negative self-talk and negative feelings becomes a potent force acting against you and will always produce negative results.

The first result will be increased tension in your muscles. Apart from a general tightening of the muscles of your neck, back and shoulders, the most significant impact is on the hands. The comfortable relaxed grip with the hands feeling as though they are working as a single unit is replaced by one expressively described by Greg Norman as 'hanging on so tightly that the knuckles are white'.

The tension in the arms, shoulders and back affects the ease with which you turn on the backswing and the way you complete your follow through. Because of the increased output of adrenaline associated with your anxiousness, every part of your swing is speeded up leading to a total loss of rhythm and tempo. To add to your distress, the uncertainty about what is going to happen to the shot often leads to an overwhelming desire to move your head too early in the downswing, known as 'looking up'.

Negative self-talk has set up a chain reaction of anxiety and tension in your body and mind, resulting in your swing becoming seriously affected. This is why I consider it so important to use the challenge exercise in dealing with this insidious and damaging thought process. Otherwise, it will keep coming back to haunt you, particularly when you are under pressure.

To recap, negative self-talk can damage your game and dealing with it involves a three-stage process:

1. **recognising** it
2. **challenging** it
3. **responding** with positive thinking

Once this sequence, which I've called 'the challenge exercise', becomes an established part of your routine, you will find that you have a more positive approach to every aspect of your golf.

CHAPTER FOUR

Visualising the Positive Game of Golf

Visualisation, or seeing pictures in your mind's eye, is a complex phenomenon which is currently creating a great deal of interest among researchers in the fields of medicine and psychology. It's a process you call on every day of your life but probably don't realise you are doing so.

To show you how important it is, if I asked you to add up 4, 11 and 16, the chances are that you would picture the numbers as I mentioned them and 'see' the final total in your mind's eye. Another example would be if I asked you to describe the ears of a Labrador dog. First, you would get a mental picture of the ears hanging close to the dog's head before describing them to me. You might also 'see' them as being black or brown, depending on which type is more familiar to you.

Both of these examples indicate how you use mental pictures based on previous experiences as a way of deciding how you're going to deal with a situation. In the first case, you 'saw' the numbers and in the second, the ears before giving your answer.

This is typical of most of the things you have to deal with in life and indicates how consistently you rely on this mental process.

In sport, this technique is an essential part of every elite athlete's training regime because it's recognised as being necessary for success. It's not difficult to understand why this process has such an impact on the way, for instance, you hit a golf shot. Recent research has shown that the brain cells you use in visualisation are exactly the same as those you use when you're actually looking at something.

So when you line up a putt on the green, for instance, your mind draws on the memory of thousands of other ones you have confronted in the past and uses this memory to decide how you should stroke it. This is the subconscious mind at work but you can also reinforce this by consciously using visualisation. Here, you deliberately direct your mind to use its visual powers so that it 'sees' the path along which you hit the ball. Your mind then computerises the input data it receives from your visualisation brain cells and decides how hard and along which line you should hit the ball.

Since visualisation is so vital in controlling many of our reactions, it is not hard to understand why it's useful in all sports. Golf, in particular, lends itself to the use of visualisation or picture imagery because of the time factor. You set the pace that you play the game and so you are in control of how much time is available to visualise the shot before playing it.

How professionals use visualisation

It's not surprising that the elite players of the game, the professional golfers, draw extensively on visualisation, especially during tournaments. Following his win in the second round of the 1994 Nations Cup at St. Andrews, Greg Norman underlined its importance:

> 'You must visualise. You must feel your shot before you execute it. If you don't, anything can happen because muscles are grooved to shots that you play. But if your mind doesn't tell your muscles what to do, they are not going to execute properly'.

When a world-ranked professional golfer like Norman extols the benefits of visualisation and the importance of the mind–body relationship, then the average club golfer should take note and make an effort to learn these techniques.

There is nothing new about the use of visualisation methods in golf. Some 20 years ago Jack Nicklaus extolled its virtues, comparing it to 'going to the movies'. He said:

> 'I never hit a shot, even in practice, without having a very sharp, in-focus picture of it in my head. It's like a color movie. First I "see" the ball where I want it to finish, nice and white and sitting up high on the bright green grass.
>
> 'Then the scene quickly changes and I "see" the ball going there: its path, trajectory, and shape, even its behavior on landing. Then there's a sort of fade-out, and the next scene shows me making the kind of swing that will turn the previous images into reality. Only at the end of this short, private, Hollywood spectacular do I select a club and step up to the ball'.

It's clear from this description by Nicklaus that he has a talent for picturing the scene and obviously uses it to its maximum.

Note how he brings refined details into his visualisation, like colour and the way in which the ball sits on the grass.

An interesting observation that I've made over many years of helping professional sportspeople is that the majority have a very high capacity to picture things in great detail and use all their sensory organs when they are visualising. So intense is this process that whenever they use it, especially during relaxation, they are able to 'hear' the appropriate sounds, experience the necessary 'feel' of a club or bat, as well as 'see' themselves performing in the correct way.

Tour professional, David Graham, explains in his book *Mental Toughness Training for Golf* that this type of all-encompassing visualisation is a key element in a successful round:

> 'Some golfers seem blessed with strong visualisation skills, while others aren't. When I'm visualising well, I see things happening in great detail. I see the path the clubhead will follow on the backswing and downswing. I can hear the "crack" of the club face meeting the ball. I see the divot flying in the air, the ball zipping to the target. This certainly has been true with me during my best performances'.

Most club professionals, too, believe that average golfers should incorporate visualisation into every shot if they want to improve their handicap. David Mercer, senior professional at The Killara Golf Club, Sydney told me that one of his major teaching points is to get golfers to go through a fixed set-up routine every time they address the ball.

It is a four-step sequence:

1. focus on the grip,

2. visualise the flight of the ball and the point on the fairway where it will land,

3. adjust the ball position in your stance

4. hit the ball.

You will notice that whereas Nicklaus uses visualisation techniques before going through his set-up, Mercer incorporates them into the routine.

This confirms my view that you should use visualisation in whatever way seems best for you. There should never be any fixed rules in using any of the techniques in this book. Each of us thinks and responds a little differently and, for this reason, you should feel free to modify any procedure so that it suits you. Trial and error will always be the best indicator when you need to make an adjustment to the way you use visualisation or any other technique.

However, as David Graham points out, some golfers have better visualisation skills than others. If you find that you are not good at visualising, rather than get upset or frustrated by your difficulties just accept that this is the way it is. One thing which should encourage you is that visualisation improves with practice.

You can help this process along by spending a few moments practising a simple technique at home:

- Sit quietly in a chair, close your eyes and try to imagine the room around you. Picture the decor, colour of the carpet, the feel of the chair material on your hands and any sounds which are present, such as the ticking of a clock.

Then open your eyes and notice how much of the surroundings you were able to 'see' when they were closed. If you were less than successful with the initial effort, repeat the procedure until you are able to get a detailed mental picture of everything around you. Incidentally, this procedure not only strengthens your ability to visualise but also acts as a form of relaxation, much like meditation.

If you have difficulty picturing your shots on the course, try using the twilight time at night to help you establish the right mood. This is the time when you are relaxed, drowsy and about to drop off to sleep, conditions which provide an ideal medium for practising mental visualisation:

- Imagine a beautifully warm, sunny day and you are playing a few holes on your home course. Play each shot in your mind from tee to green as if you were there. As your imagery improves, you will find you're able to become more detailed in what you picture. You 'feel' the warmth of the sun on your back, the pressure of your hands on the grip. You 'hear' the sound of the clubhead striking the ball and 'see' the ball in flight, settling exactly where you intended it to go.

Apart from improving your ability to visualise, this exercise acts as a wonderful, drug-free way of putting you to sleep.

How to use visualisation

You may be thinking that it's all very well for professional golfers to use these mental imagery techniques but what's in it for you? This is not unreasonable. Whenever someone suggests a new approach which purports to improve your game, always tune into your inner radio station WII FM (What's In It For Me). Often, the things suggested prove to have little merit but I can confidently predict that if you use visualisation and the other mind techniques described, it will make an enormous difference to your standard of golf. It is, in effect, a reprogramming technique for your mind and helps establish a more successful and consistent way of hitting the ball.

There are two ways you can tune into the pictures in your mind:

1. Use it during a game to mentally 'see' the shot you're about to play.

2. Use a form of visual rehearsal. This is where you go through a series of scenes in your mind in which you imagine yourself correctly playing a particular hole or shot. It can be done either when you're sitting quietly or, preferably, when you are relaxed.

Using visualisation during a game

Most professional golfers will tell you that they always use this technique when playing in tournaments. Jenny Sevil is a firm believer:

> 'It's important. You've always got to know what you want to do before you do it, especially with putting. That's the time people get really tense. I take myself away from myself and picture the line of the putt and the ball going into the hole. Then I go ahead and do it'.

Similarly, tour professional Ian Baker-Finch uses this technique. He says: 'I picture the course, the direction of the wind, the hazards and the best position to be for my next shot'. You will notice a link here between visualisation and the technique of using your mental camera lenses to change your focus of concentration. This is to be expected because, as I mentioned earlier, you use exactly the same part of the brain whether you're looking at something or mentally picturing it. This shows how each psychological aspect of your game, including visualisation, can be seen as one piece of a complex mental jigsaw. Being able to play consistent and satisfactory golf will depend ultimately on how well you fit the pieces together.

Even though visualisation is an essential part of the professional's game, it's curious that the technique is so rarely used by handicap golfers. It may be that the average player has so much to think about when setting up that either they forget about it, or they simply have never considered using it. Whichever category you fall in, I would suggest that now is the time for change. If you have never used visualisation procedures, you'll need to remind yourself about them with each shot you play until the technique is a regular part of your game. It's worth remembering that golf habits only develop through repetition.

Seeing your game

To get started, make a conscious decision before every round that you're going to use visualisation each time you settle over a shot. You will find the habit is reinforced if you use the technique during practice, a point emphasised by teaching professional Greg Hohnen. He suggests that instead of hitting practice balls in a repetitive and mindless fashion, you should imagine you're playing a round and that you're aiming at a specific target on one of the golf holes. If you are practising with a three iron, for example, pretend that you are hitting to the 18th green and picture the type of shot you need to play. Visualising during practice will enhance your ability to use it when you're under the pressure of competition.

Begin on the first tee by seeing the shots you are going to play. No matter how many thoughts intrude, decide that you are only going to focus on a few and one will be visualisation.

Establish a routine. You could follow the steps suggested by professional David Mercer of grip, visualisation, ball position and stroke, or you may prefer to develop your own. Either way, visualisation should be an integral part of the set-up ritual.

Next, picture the ball flying off the clubface, the shot in flight and then 'see' the ball settling exactly where you want it to finish. This process only takes a few seconds but it's such an important part of your game. It means your mind is controlling the muscles necessary to produce a good result.

This process is even more crucial the closer you get to the green. Whether you are hitting a long iron or pitching wedge, be sure to 'see' the ball landing either on or short of the green and running to the pin. With short pitch shots, you need to picture the exact spot where you want the ball to land if it's to finish within easy putting distance of the hole. So often you'll see other golfers hit the ball to the fringe, leaving themselves an unattainable putt. Whenever this happens, you can be sure they have failed to tap into the 'programming' effect that visualisation has on their inner computer, the brain.

I have emphasised the need to practise these techniques until they become a habit. Golf, I believe, is not so much a sport as a discipline. Success will always depend on how much time and effort you are prepared to invest in the game. As Gary Player once said when an observer quipped about how lucky he was when his bunker shot finished in the hole: 'Funny isn't it. The more I practise, the luckier I get'. This is true of all facets of the game.

Mentally rehearsing your game

You have probably experienced occasions in the past when you needed to set aside time to dwell upon some issue in your life, such as confronting a difficult family situation or speaking to a public group. You might go through the mental exercise of picturing yourself dealing with the potential problem successfully. This is where you are using your mind to rehearse a situation so that you can cope with it when it happens.

In precisely the same way, you can use this technique to improve your golf swing or any aspect of your game. This form of mental rehearsal is widely used by athletes in all sports including golf. It's another means of 'programming' the mental computer so that it 'knows' the correct way to respond in a particular situation. Once the details of how you should play a particular hole are fixed in your mind, you will draw on that imagined experience at the right time and use it as a 'template' so that you hit the ball correctly.

The aim of this technique is to picture a golfing scene in as much detail as possible. Select a situation you would like to improve or one that has been difficult for you in the past. You have a choice. You can incorporate your rehearsal into a full relaxation session. Practising it when you are in a calm state of mind will make every picture more vivid and realistic. This gives the whole effect more power. However, not everyone can devote time to relaxing, so you can also do the exercises sitting quietly in a chair with your eyes closed.

Rehearsing the problem hole

Have you ever experienced the situation of finding that there is one hole on a course that is your bête noire? No matter how you approach that hole, it always seems to get the better of you. After you've experienced many failures playing it, your confidence is undermined and you are convinced that you will never succeed on this hole.

This is the ideal situation to test the effectiveness of mental rehearsal. In your relaxed or quiet state, try to capture a detailed mental picture of yourself playing each shot from tee to green.

Imagine you're addressing the ball. You check your grip and notice how comfortable the club feels in your hands as you take a practice waggle. You picture yourself visualising the shot you're going to play (known as creating a picture within a picture), taking a slow, smooth backswing with a full turn of the shoulders and then releasing the clubhead into the ball on your downswing.

Next visualise the ball flying through the air on a perfect trajectory and finishing in an ideal position on the fairway. Repeat this routine with each shot, finally sinking the putt to make par.

If you are still doubtful that visualisation can change the way you play a hole, be assured that the technique has been tested and found to be extremely successful. However, it will take many repetitions of the mental rehearsal process before you can expect complete success.

Unfortunately, my experience of helping sportspeople has shown that most of them anticipate instant gratification. Golfers are no exception, so I suggest you practise the techniques with patience. There are no magic wand answers to dealing with problems stemming from the mind and, as with most good things in life, you will have to work at it.

Rehearsing your swing

Another way of using mental rehearsal is to visualise your swing in detail. This is never as easy as you might think and particularly if you have a swing deficiency. Nevertheless, the mind is like a complex computer and stores so much data including all the details of your swing and any problems you may have developed. Your teaching professional can usually identify these and suggest corrections, but a new swing pattern will still depend on how much effort you put into practice.

One valuable way of speeding up the change is by using mental rehearsal. Some golfers prefer to picture their faulty swing and then imagine themselves swinging as they have been taught by their pro. Others visualise themselves swinging in an ideal way. Whichever technique you try, make a point of 'seeing' the swing in as much detail as you can. It helps to visualise even such minor items as your golf shoes, the colour of your golf bag or the trees and plants around you.

Working on these details will help to increase your sense of mental awareness, which is usually less well developed than you realise. If you have any doubts about this, try to recall the colour of the furnishings or carpet in your golf clubhouse or in a friend's home. Even though you may have been there many times, the chances are that you will be uncertain of the answers.

To get the most out of mental rehearsal techniques, you should reinforce it with actual physical practice. If your problem is the way you play a particular hole, go out and play it several times and then rehearse it visually in your mind. This approach of alternating mental and physical rehearsal is an effective way of 'fixing' the desired changes into your subconscious so that your swing becomes consistent.

Golf is very much a game of 'what you "see" is what you get'. Once you bring your 'seeing' mechanism into play, you will be surprised by how much your score improves.

CHAPTER FIVE

Improving Your General Approach

There are many situations in golf that can cause problems. In this chapter, I focus on several of these situations and suggest ways of dealing with them. The aim is to give you specific hints that you can follow when you encounter similar problems during a game. All are based on sound, practical psychological principles and are easy to work into your normal golf routine.

The problem areas we will concentrate on are:

- Pre-game anxiety
- Pre-game warm-up
- Sharpening visualisation skills
- Changing your concentration
- Coping with on-course tension
- Pacing yourself and your game
- How to enjoy a round of golf

However, no matter how keen your are to build these techniques into your game, you must guard against overloading your mind with too many thoughts. In many golfing situations, you are already overburdened with thoughts about what you should be doing with your grip, your swing and your stance.

Pre-game anxiety

A common problem when your mind is overburdened with worries is the feeling that, no matter how hard you try, you can't settle your mind to golf. This feeling emanates from anxiety and usually starts before you get to the course. By the time you arrive and unload your clubs, the anxiousness can be so severe that you can be at a complete loss as to how you are going to cope with your game.

Here are few practical steps to follow which will help restore your equanimity and set your game off on the right foot.

On the way to the course, start the process of slowing things down mentally by concentrating on breathing through the nose:

1. Make each inhalation a long, slow and complete one lasting about 10 seconds.

2. As you breathe in, you should feel as though your waist is being pushed sideways. This indicates that you are using the correct diaphragmatic breathing, which not only brings more air into your lungs but also helps you become more relaxed. (Chest breathing can actually increase tension and yet it is the type practised by most people.)

3. Pause for 5 seconds until you feel the need to exhale.

4. Breathe out slowly as though you are trying to empty your lungs completely. This part of the cycle will take about 10 seconds.

5. Again, pause for about 5 seconds until you feel the need to repeat the cycle.

6. Your aim is to establish a slow, steady rhythm in your breathing so that you fit in about 5 or 6 complete cycles each minute.

7. Work at developing the sequence of a slow in-breath, pause, slow out-breath, pause. Continue to do this for about 5 minutes before your game.

If anxious thoughts or worries disturb your concentration and interfere with the rhythm of your breathing, think of 'CALM' with each out-breath so that the word fills the whole exhalation cycle.

I suggest that you practise this technique on your own with as little distraction around as possible. You may find it helpful, as part of this process, to use visualisation as a means of aiding tension release. Each time you breathe out, imagine you are pushing neck and shoulder tension through the tips of your fingers until your hands feel relaxed and comfortable.

Pre-game warm-up

It is surprising how few handicap golfers bother to practise before a round. Often they haven't even taken a club from the bag since the last time they played but still expect to take up where they left off the previous week. It is simply not feasible for your muscles to perform as they should unless you take the necessary steps to retrain and stretch them by hitting practice balls. This is the main reason why tournament professionals spend hours on the practice fairway before competition.

A pre-game warm-up loosens your muscles and minimises the chance of injury. It also enables you to regroove your swing and gives you an opportunity to sharpen your visualisation skills.

Grip tension

Start your practice with a reassessment of your grip and the grip pressure. Estimate how tightly you are holding the club by noting how easy it is to 'feel' the weight of the clubhead when you make a small backwards and forwards waggle.

If you're unable to 'feel' the clubhead in your abbreviated swing, it indicates you're holding on too tightly. Take a few moments break from your practice session and concentrate on breathing slowly through the nose, again getting the feeling you're releasing tension through your fingertips as you breathe out. It usually takes no more than a few minutes of this exercise to restore a relaxed feel to your grip.

Establish rhythm

To help develop rhythm in your swing and at the same time relax your muscles, stand with your feet together and, with a middle iron in your hands, pace your backswing so that it matches a long, slow in-breath. Then take a short pause in your breathing before beginning your downswing as you slowly breathe out.

The backswing doesn't have to be a full shoulder turn to be effective. Taking the club to the horizontal is sufficient. After repeating this action for several minutes, you'll feel a looseness coming into your muscles and a sense of timing coming into your swing.

Perform this exercise without the ball at first. When you have attained a relaxed rhythm, try hitting several shots with the same breathing and swing action. The distance or direction of the shots is immaterial, the aim is to establish a relaxed, comfortable swing pattern.

Initiate visualisation

Before heading off to the first tee, end the practice session by using visualisation. Teaching professional Greg Hohnen suggests spending the last few minutes of practice hitting with your driver. As you do so, imagine you are hitting off the first tee, picture the type of shot you want to play and the ball finishing exactly where it should. This will ensure your mind is already attuned to the task ahead when it comes time to hit your first drive of the round.

Finish the pre-game warm-up by spending a few moments using slow, rhythmical, nasal breathing to reduce any excess arousal that may have developed. You can do this as you walk to the first tee.

Sharpening visualisation skills

Although most people bring visualisation into their everyday life, few seem to apply the principles in a conscious way. Golfers are no different and, in my experience, most fail to call on these valuable techniques when they are playing.

Many golfers may have difficulty mentally picturing things but, fortunately, you don't have to be able to visualise in great detail in order to achieve success with this approach. It might be the case that you can only picture a scene as if you were watching it on video or you simply think of it without getting any real mental pictures. Whatever your ability, visualisation allows you to 'program' the correct swing for any particular shot.

There are two ways you can sharpen your visualisation skills. The first exercise you perform on the course and the second is a form of mental rehearsal that you practise quietly when you are at home.

Visualising on the course

1. Focus on your grip and make any adjustments to it which ensures your hands feel as though they are working as one unit.

2. Set your alignment accurately, for it determines the direction of your shot. If your alignment is out of plumb then, no matter how well you hit the ball, the result will be less than desirable.

To set correct alignment, stand behind the ball and look along the line of flight. Choose a small object such as a leaf, worm cast or tuft of grass which is no more than a metre from your ball and lies on the direct 'flight path' between your ball and where you want your shot to finish. Lay the clubface on the ground so that it faces your chosen 'marker' and as you adjust your feet so that they are in the correct position with the ball, check that you haven't disturbed the alignment by ensuring the clubface still points to the small target in front of you.

(Cautionary note: You can't deliberately place an object in front of your ball to indicate the line of play—Rule 8-2a of the Rules of Golf. However, this doesn't preclude your using something that is already there, such as a leaf.)

3. Now is the ideal time to introduce visualisation. Your mind is no longer encumbered by the set-up routine and you can spend the next few moments picturing the type of shot you're going to hit, whether you will shape it with a fade or a draw and whether it will be a low or high shot.

4. Imagine where you want the ball to land and where it should finish. This depends on how much 'run' and slope there is on the fairway.

5. When you have finished the visualisation process, put complete trust in your subconscious and carry out your normal swing. The benefit of going through this set routine is that each facet of it serves to 'program' your mind to react correctly once you start your swing.

Picturing your game

A feature of mental rehearsal is that you can practise it anywhere. Although I recommend you do it in a quiet environment such as your home, it is equally effective if you practise in the office, in the garden, travelling on public transport or when walking. Using it in these everyday situations has the added advantage of positively utilising time that would otherwise be wasted.

1. Settle yourself in a comfortable chair and spend the first few moments concentrating on slow, regular breathing until you feel relaxed and at ease. The reason it is better for you to be relaxed is that it helps your mind intensify mental pictures of a scene.

2. When you feel relaxed, close your eyes and think of a golf hole that has caused you problems in the recent past. Try to visualise the layout of the hole from tee to green, including any bunkers, the slope of the fairway and the position of the pin on the green. It is as though you are following a slow motion view from a helicopter, similar to those shown on television during tournaments. This may take several minutes to complete and the aim is to give your mind a more accurate idea of where each shot should finish.

3. Imagine standing on the tee and going through your pre-shot routine, including visualising the type of shot you want to play. Here, you are imagining yourself visualising (forming a picture within a picture). If you have developed this ability, you will have a detailed recall of all aspects of your set-up and swing.

4. Imagine how the club 'feels' in your hands, the sense of weight distribution in your feet when you are addressing the ball, the weight transfer during your backswing, a complete shoulder turn with your wrists cocking naturally and a forward swing that brings the clubhead into perfect contact with the ball. Imagine your weight transferring quite automatically to the outside of your front foot and your hands finishing in a high position. Because your aim is to picture yourself playing each shot in an ideal way, imagine each part of your swing as being perfect.

5. When you have completed the visualisation of your swing, 'see' the flight of the ball, the point where it lands and rolls to a stop in an ideal position on the fairway. A word of advice: be sure to visualise a result that is within your capabilities. It would be unrealistic to picture yourself driving a ball 250 metres when the reality is that you can only hit it 200 metres. Nevertheless, this doesn't preclude visualising it finishing in an ideal spot at that distance.

6. Picture yourself walking to your next shot, perhaps adjusting your mental focusing lens to a wide-angle plane. Imagine a gentle breeze and the way you will play the shot. In mental rehearsal, your mind should be tuned to taking in fine details. It is always actively involved in some feature of your game even when you picture yourself walking between shots. The purpose of this is to train your mind to use all the intervals instead of viewing it as 'dead' time.

7. Repeat the set-up and swing imagery in detail with each shot until you reach the green.

8. Picture the ball at various distances from the pin and 'see' yourself coping with each situation in an ideal way (putting techniques will be dealt with in a special segment later).

9. Finally, imagine you have parred the hole and you are looking back down the fairway with a sense of satisfaction before making your way to the next tee.

As with any aspect of golf practice, the more you use these techniques, the greater the benefits to your game. They require no more than 10 minutes of your time and if you are prepared to do four or five sessions a week, you will have developed a much more positive approach to your game.

Changing your concentration

Good concentration is a critical factor in golf but the process is far more complex than you may think. It may require you to take a fresh look at the way in which focus affects concentration.

You need to call on two different types of mental focus when you are playing golf. As we noted previously, you need a narrow, intense focus when you're setting up for a shot but you need to switch to a much wider focus when you're walking between shots.

In Chapter 1, I explained a simple way of developing the correct focusing approach during a round by considering the two types of concentration as lenses of a camera. The narrow focus is like a close-up lens and the broader focus like a wide-angle lens. The advantage of this approach is that it enables you to train the mind to switch easily from one focus to the other, just as you would change your camera lenses to suit a particular scene you want to photograph.

Using your camera lens

It is important to adopt a technique that will help you switch your concentration easily. What you want to avoid is being trapped in the wrong focus at the wrong time. A common example of this is when you find yourself still thinking about some aspect of the last hole you played (wide focus) rather than concentrating on your grip and the set-up for your next shot (narrow focus):

1. Whenever you set up to address the ball, whether it's on the tee or fairway, make a point of consciously switching on your close-up lens. You can do this, if you wish, by silently 'telling' yourself to do so. Initially, it may be necessary to do this with every shot but after a while, it becomes more of an automatic response.
2. Focus down, first on your grip, second on ball position and alignment and finally, on visualising the shot you need to play. Select a small object close by as your alignment guide to keep your focus of attention on a narrow band rather than having it disrupted by constantly looking at a distant target.
3. Once you have played your shot, make a point of changing to your wide-angle mental lens. A useful reminder could be the act of returning your club to the bag or replacing the cover.
4. Maintain this wide focus of concentration as you walk to your next shot and use this time productively to assess any wind

direction, the position of hazards or the type of shot you need to play, especially if you are in a difficult situation, such as beneath tree branches. This broad view of things enables your mind to start work on 'programming' how you are going to play the next shot and prevents it from having to deal with an overwhelming number of thoughts when you reach the ball.

Using a cue

It is helpful to build into your game a cue or mental 'bellringer' that will remind you to switch to the appropriate mental focusing lens you need in order to deal with the immediate situation.

Always use a cue that is already part of your game and the most obvious and constant one is the ball. Develop a habit of consciously reminding yourself to switch on your close-up lens whenever you address the ball. In that way, the ball becomes an integral part of your narrowed focus of concentration.

We have noted that a club can also serve as a cue. Whenever you take a club from the bag, this can jog your memory to change to your narrow focus lens. In the same way, replacing the club in the bag can be the signal for you to open up your focus once again.

Using a cue mechanism makes it less likely that you will forget to change mental lenses when you are under pressure. A classic situation where it is often easy to forget to make the necessary lens change is when you're playing short approach shots to the green. Once you have your mental 'bellringer' fixed into your game, these situations are no longer a problem.

In brief, 'fix' the technique into your mind by consciously associating two things: the cue itself, and the narrowing of your focus. You will find that your mind becomes conditioned to react to this mental trigger even in the most pressured situations.

Finally, get yourself in good physical shape. It is difficult to maintain concentration when you are tired. If you are serious about improving your performance, make a decision to take a brisk half-hour walk at least three times a week. Not only will this stop you tiring when you are out on the course but it will also do wonders for your body, general health and state of mind.

Coping with on-course tension

Tension is a result of anxiety and it can strike at any time during your game. It takes surprisingly little disruption to your thinking for the tension and tightness cycle to start. The one thing that can be guaranteed whenever you feel tense is the dramatic and damaging effect it will have on your swing and your score.

Recognise tension

Like most golfers, you are probably unwilling to admit that you might suffer from tension on the course. This overt denial explains why tension is often well entrenched before you recognise it. Obviously, you can't change until you are aware of what is happening and there are some tell-tale indicators to watch out for. If you are in doubt about whether you are tense, the following questions posed to yourself will give you a quick and accurate answer.

- Am I swinging faster than usual?
- Does my grip feel too tight?
- Is there any tightness in my neck, shoulders or arms during set-up?
- Am I finding it difficult to complete my full backswing?
- Is my mind filled with all sorts of negative thoughts for no particular reason?

Replace tension with positive thinking

We have identified the principal psychological factor associated with tension as negative thinking. If you have hit a bad shot that has landed you in trouble it is easy to feel your game has fallen apart and your mind can become a mass of negative thoughts. You must counteract this tendency and replace it with thoughts that help you adopt a more positive approach. We have demonstrated that the challenge exercise is a good method for dealing with negative thoughts by replacing them with positive thinking.

Use the challenge exercise to carry on an internal debate with yourself until you recognise that, not only are the thoughts illogical, but they also create a great deal of tension at a time when you least need it. Pose a challenge question such as: 'So I played a poor shot and I'm in a difficult situation because of it. Does it mean that it's impossible for me to get out of these trees?'.

Once you have counteracted negative self-talk, instil positive, realistic thoughts: 'I can play a safe shot out of here. It doesn't matter that I have to sacrifice a shot. I'll play a low shot off my back foot and aim for that wide gap between the trees. That'll put me back on the fairway and I still have an outside chance to make par'.

Relaxation cue

It is important to have a technique that you can call on when you are starting to feel tense or anxious on the course. It must be simple to apply and effective in producing an immediate sense of relief from your problems. You can use a relaxation cue that can be incorporated into your breathing exercise. Use the word 'CALM' for your cue. This acts as an indirect signal to your mind to relax. It is preferable to the more obvious word 'relax' because the latter is likely to engender a desire to try to relax rather than just letting it happen.

When you are aware that tension is starting to trouble you, begin slow nasal breathing similar to that discussed in the relief of pre-game anxiety. This form of breathing can be performed while you are walking and requires no special time or intense effort. Follow this sequence.

Take a long, slow in-breath through the nose, pause for 5 seconds and let out that breath in the same slow fashion. This should be followed by another 5 second pause before repeating the cycle.

The rate at which you breathe should be such that, if you are walking normally, you would take about 12 paces from the start of one cycle to the start of the next.

After you've established a regular breathing pattern, you can use a relaxation cue. Each time you breathe out, think of the word 'CALM' so that it fills the whole or most of the exhalation phase.

You will notice that, after using it a few times, feelings of tension ease in your neck and shoulders.

Repeat the exercise until you feel comfortable again. You will find it useful to reinforce the cue in a variety of situations around the course. Practise it when there is a break, such as when you are on the green or when waiting your turn to hit from the tee or fairway. The more you practise it, the more effectively it will act as a 'trigger mechanism' for the mind and body to relax.

Pacing yourself and your game

One aspect of golf that players rarely consider is the pace at which they play the game. Some play so slowly that they create a 'log-jam' on the course. This is not only thoughtless behaviour towards fellow golfers but also breaches Rule 6-7 of the Rules of Golf.

Golf is a game that still relies on players following a code of etiquette. It is what makes the game different from many other sports. Playing your round at an acceptable pace is not only good manners but good for your overall playing rhythm.

But few golfers are able to set the correct pace for themselves during a round. They start with the best intentions of moving along in a steady, unhurried fashion but then something happens which disturbs their equilibrium and, suddenly, they do everything too fast.

Whenever this happens, you should be aware of the symptoms of anxiety. Something has occurred which has set your adrenaline flowing and it is this internal chemical that is responsible for your hasty reactions. The cause of the adrenaline release is anxiety and everything, including your walk, swing and even your decision-making becomes speeded up. Once this process has begun, it is impossible to counteract by willpower alone.

If you have any doubts about the impact anxiety has on a golfer's pace, watch carefully when one of your group hits a shot into a trouble spot such as dense trees. In most cases, their usual steady walk to the next shot is replaced by a violent tug at their buggy as they head off at great speed to find out what dreadful fate has befallen them. By the time they reach the ball, their mind is full of negative self-talk and, without giving the next shot any sort of reasonable consideration, they add to their problems by taking a wild and hasty swipe at the ball.

Usually, this lands them in an even worse predicament and the result is that they use up far more time and extra strokes than if they had adopted a slow, relaxed approach to the situation. It's a classic example of that old saying: 'more haste, less speed'. The solution lies in tuning into signs that indicate you're speeding up too much, and in using specific techniques to restore your equilibrium.

Setting the pace

Make a conscious decision before your round that you're going to do everything at a constant pace. This includes the rate at which you swing, how you walk to your next shot and your approach to playing out of trouble situations.

The signs which will indicate your adrenaline is starting to flow too much are:

- Your grip may tighten.

- Your breathing and swing quicken.
- You walk more rapidly than normal.

Be ready to tune into these indicators and recognise the damage they can do. They are warning signs that you are becoming anxious or worried. The following steps can alleviate stress and re-establish your pacing:

1. When you're walking to your ball on the fairway, breathe slowly and easily through the nose, using the breathing as a guide to your pace.
2. If your previous stroke has landed your ball in a hazard or a problem situation such as trees, deliberately alter your pace so that you appear to be moving even slower than usual. In fact, because of the increased adrenaline in your system, you will probably be walking more quickly than you realise.
3. If you find your ball has landed in a difficult spot, stop for a few moments and take stock of the situation, considering what type of recovery shot you can safely play. During this temporary respite, take three or four slow, deep breaths and think 'CALM'. This will help release tension and allow you time to plan your next shot.
4. Play a shot that has the greatest chance of success, even if this means playing sideways or backwards. You may be tempted to play the 'impossible shot' rather than the safe one, viewing it as a challenge. Even those golfers with exceptional skills often come to grief with this approach. The reality is that it is better to accept that you have sacrificed one shot

to get your ball back into play rather than challenge the odds of probability and find that the cost is even higher.

5. Check the pace you walk and the speed of your swing from time to time throughout the game. Anxiety is such an insidious process that it often affects you gradually, leading to an overall increase in tempo in all your movements. If you sense that you have increased your pace or your timing is off, use your breathing as a means of bringing it quickly under control.

How to enjoy a round of golf

In spite of the frustrations in playing golf, there is no doubt that it fulfils an important role in many people's lives. It serves as a break away from the everyday pressures we all experience these days and it is a wonderful way of meeting other people.

However, the social aspects of golf may not be fulfilling if you feel stressed or have personal problems on your mind. If you feel grumpy and uncommunicative, you will finish the game with a sense of dissatisfaction. More to the point, you are unlikely to be a welcome playing companion.

We all know that personalities differ. One day you will play with someone who is a total extrovert, a person whose normal behaviour is to talk, laugh and crack jokes incessantly. The next day you may be teamed with a person who is introverted and makes only a few comments throughout the round.

How you deal with these quite different personalities can easily become a deciding factor in how well you play and the degree of enjoyment you get out of the game. You may be either one of these two personalities and approach the game from either of these vantage points.

Whether you are an outgoing or introverted person should not become so important that it determines how much you enjoy your game. Golfers are an understanding and forgiving group and generally allow for the personal idiosyncrasies of their fellow players. Nevertheless, it's worth bearing in mind that their tolerance will only stretch so far before they react to something they perceive to be unacceptable behaviour.

There are a few rules which can make your time on the course a pleasant interlude and one where you can enjoy the companionship of other golfers.

People problems

Some people like to talk the whole time they're walking between shots. Often, they use this as a means of keeping their own tension under control but, unfortunately, fellow golfers sometimes find this incessant chatter distracting and irritating. This is not surprising and is one reason why you rarely see tournament professionals talking to anyone but their caddy while they're playing.

If you feel distracted by a partner's talk, rather than create a confrontation over the issue, it would be easier and kinder to the other person if you said:

> 'I probably seem a bit preoccupied and quiet today. I hope you don't mind if I don't talk very much. It's just that, when I do, my concentration seems to fall apart'.

Most golfers will respond to this gentle request in a positive manner and direct their thoughts to their own game, limiting their conversation to appropriate times. Sometimes a quiet, almost lack of response, approach can tone down even the most active 'talker'.

Make a conscious decision before each round that, no matter how aggravating your partner's behaviour, you will lose yourself into your game rather than lose your temper. You may wonder why you need to make this form of self-commitment. The reason is that not everyone you play with is going to exhibit the same approach to golf as yourself. Some people, for instance, are highly competitive and often adopt a win-at-all-costs approach to golf, usually coupled with a frenzied desire to bet on just about any aspect of the game. If you are not a competitive person and feel uncomfortable with this, it is perfectly acceptable to decline to be involved. Make your position clear when the issue is first raised and you will be respected if you choose not to participate.

Relaxation problems

If you have some personal worries in your life, it is too easy to carry them with you on to the course. You can counteract this tendency by tuning into your negative self-talk as suggested in Chapter 3. Do this before you start the game and you should ask yourself the challenge question:

- Will it help my problems if I continue to worry about them right throughout this round?

This challenge will soon convince you that no amount of worry will resolve anything.

It also provides an opportunity to instil positive thoughts:

- OK. So it would make more sense if I go out today just to enjoy my golf. I might not play as well as I would like but that's not important. I'll keep my mind focused on every shot, relax and let things happen.

If tension or anxious feelings threaten to make you an unwelcome playing partner, use your relaxation cue to settle down. Think 'CALM' each time you breathe out until you feel a perceptible easing of tension in your muscles and a reduction in the flow of negative thoughts through your mind.

I suggest you use the relaxation technique while you're getting ready to go to the course and follow this with your pre-game practice or warm-up routines. Once you have become familiar with these, you should incorporate ways of reducing first tee jitters by using the mental camera techniques for improving your concentration. By the time you've reached this point, you will be ready to introduce visualisation into your game.

If this is a new approach for you, it will be necessary to remind yourself to practise it with every shot, and it may take several rounds of golf before it becomes second nature to you. As a more relaxed playing companion, you will certainly find greater enjoyment in the game.

CHAPTER SIX

Problem Solving Course Guide

An unusual aspect of golf is that some situations can create excessive feelings of concern, anxiety and even fear in many players. A few of these problems, such as bunkers, trees and water hazards, are specifically designed to make the course more challenging by introducing an element of doubt into your game. But other problems are creations of your own imagination. Once negative self-talk takes hold, minor concerns can become very real mental hazards. No matter which type of problem troubles you there is always a solution providing, of course, you know what appropriate measures to take. In this Chapter, I will show you how you can deal effectively with:

- First tee anxiety.
- Playing out of bunkers.
- Fear of water hazards.
- Putting to save shots.

First tee anxiety

First tee anxiety is the most common problem confronting golfers. Few players can admit to never having felt nervous when preparing to drive off the first tee. In some respects, it can be the most important shot of the day because it often sets the tone for what happens with the rest of your game. What makes it doubly hard is that you are under pressure to perform well at a time when you may not have had much chance to loosen-up or even adapt your mind to golf-related matters.

To add to your discomfort, the first tee is usually near the clubhouse and professional's shop so that there is a constant stream of people on hand to observe your performance. It may be some consolation to know that even a tour-hardened professional such as Jack Nicklaus admits to having first tee nerves. Interestingly, it's a problem that never seems to disappear no matter how long you've played the game.

Coping with this problem is vital if your game is to become more satisfying and successful. Managing this situation can be seen as a four-step process:

- loosening your mind and body,
- nullifying negative self-talk,
- narrowing your concentration,
- using the positive powers of visualisation.

Loosening your mind and body

The most obvious way of loosening-up is to spend some time hitting balls on the practice fairway or in the practice net. This, coupled with your mental preparation on your way to the course should be enough to ensure a more relaxed feeling at the first tee. But what if you haven't had time to practise, which happens when you lead a busy lifestyle? This is when you need a quick and effective technique that releases excess tension.

Controlled breathing

As you are waiting your turn to hit off the first tee, take three or four slow breaths through the nose. Each time you breathe out, consciously let your shoulders sag as you breathe away tension. Feel the ease flowing right down to your fingertips so that your arms and hands are loose and relaxed.

Another effective way of relaxing is to clench your fists as you breathe in and unclench the fists as you breathe out. You will feel yourself releasing the tension from the arms and shoulders. Repeat the technique for several minutes or until all tension has dissipated.

If your mind keeps wandering to thoughts unrelated to golf, incorporate a relaxation cue into your breathing. Whenever you breathe out, think of the word 'RELEASE'. Some people prefer to 'see' the word as they silently say it to themselves, while others think of a peaceful scene for a few moments. Whatever method you choose, the net result is that your mind will be freed of bothersome thoughts so that you can focus it more easily on the task in hand, the first tee shot.

Take a few slow practice swings with your feet together and coordinate your in-breath with the backswing and your out-breath with the forward swing. It's not necessary to take the shaft of the club past the horizontal with either swing direction because the purpose of the technique is to relax your body while, at the same time, helping create a sense of coordination between your hands, arms and the club.

Nullifying negative thoughts

I have emphasised throughout the book how negative thinking is a major opponent in golf. Understandably, you may find it hard to accept that your mind can be the most powerful element controlling your game but, in fact, it creates more problems for you than the course or your swing.

You may find it hard, at first, to recognise that many of the things you are 'saying' to yourself are negative. Negative thoughts frequently form part of your normal thinking during your set-up, and are often well concealed in other thoughts about how you are going to play the shot:

- I'm going to try and swing easy with this shot.
- Nothing forced.
- I hope that slice doesn't come in again.
- My swing doesn't feel right today.
- What if I hit it out-of-bounds?

The general rule is to assume that negative thinking will try to be present whenever you are in a pressure situation, such as hitting off the first tee. Acknowledging the potential problem gives you a head start in dealing with it quickly. If you challenge your negative thoughts immediately, instead of playing a horror shot, you will be able to hit your drive with ease and confidence.

Here is a typical dialogue:

- I must stay down on this shot and keep my head still.
- That's a negative thought isn't it?
- What I'm really telling myself is that my head is definitely going to move, no matter what I do.
- But nothing is forcing me to move my head.
- It's just that I get anxious about how the shot has worked out.
- I'll swing easily and get a full shoulder turn before I start down and just wait and see how it turns out.
- I know that works because it's done so before.

Make a commitment to yourself that you will never let negative self-talk go unchallenged even if it means walking off the tee and taking a few moments to recover your composure. Remind yourself that you can control your thoughts rather than have them control you.

Narrowing your concentration

One of the many troubling effects of feeling anxious or excessively nervous is that your mind is more susceptible to being distracted by unimportant sounds and thoughts. This can happen when you are on the first tee where maintaining a narrow focus of concentration on your grip, alignment and swing is so important.

If you recognise that you are easily distracted, then be prepared to consciously switch to your close-up mental focusing lens. This approach, coupled with specific positive thoughts, enables you to focus on essentials and exclude troublesome distractions.

The following examples of positive thinking will help you:

- I know that other people are watching but they're entitled to do that. It's not that they're curious or want me to play a bad shot. They're stopping out of courtesy. Now that it's my turn to hit, I'm going to focus on my grip. Yes it feels comfortable and relaxed and my hands feel as if they're working as a unit.
- Now I'll concentrate on my alignment and ball position. Everything seems OK there.
- I'll bring the club back slowly, get a full shoulder turn and swing easily through the ball. I know that'll make a big difference to how well I hit this shot.

Tune into your visual powers

Beating first tee nerves and ensuring you hit a good drive also means using visualisation. The technique should be familiar to you by now. Develop a detailed picture in your mind of the flight and path of the ball and the point where it is going to finish. It should be part of your set-up routine for any shot but particularly before your drive off the first tee.

Professional golfers often differ about where it should be fitted into their swing preparation. Some, like Nicklaus, prefer to start the set-up routine with visualisation. Others fit it in after focusing on grip and alignment. I believe it is best done at the end of your set-up routine, the reason being that the last mental picture you form before you swing is the one which has the most profound impact on your shot.

I suggest the following steps for visualising:

1. **After going through your correct thinking and focusing routines, form a mental picture of the clubhead making contact with the ball on your forward swing and 'see' the ball flying off the tee on an ideal trajectory.**
2. **Picture, in your mind's eye, the line of flight of the ball and 'watch' it in as much detail as you can manage.**
3. **Imagine the point on the fairway where you want the ball to land and any roll you anticipate may occur.**

In visualising this, be realistic and avoid choosing an image that is beyond your abilities. In other words, if you know that your maximum driving distance is, say, 200 metres, then that is the image you should develop.

Your golfing potential is controlled by many factors including the genes you inherited, the extent of your coaching and how much you practise. The principal reason for learning and using mind-control techniques is to remove the negative psychological barriers that will interfere with your ability to realise your potential. Don't underestimate how important this is—most golfers rarely play close to their true potential because of the limitations imposed by their mind.

Playing out of bunkers

A hazard which seems to create a lot of anxiety in the mind of many golfers is the bunker. It is specifically designed to add greater challenge to a hole and, in that respect, it certainly succeeds. However, the problems of playing out of this hazard are not caused by the nature of the sand or the depth of the bunker. They come from the negative perceptions you have implanted in your mind and which begin the moment you see your ball heading in the general direction of the bunker.

Even though the bunker shot is not a difficult one to play, this does not ease the average golfer's concerns. As any professional will tell you, it's the only time you don't have to make actual contact with the ball. So why do bunker shots create so much fear and trepidation in many golfers?

There are several explanations for this. The fact that you don't have to make direct contact with the ball, may, in itself, create uncertainty. Because it's an unusual type of shot, most golfers don't spend much time practising hitting from a bunker. Yet the ability to play recovery shots seems to be the major feature that distinguishes a low marker from a long handicap golfer. This doesn't happen by chance.

Professionals and low handicap amateurs spend considerable time practising how to recover from difficult positions, including bunkers. The obvious answer to improving your confidence and expertise in bunkers is, therefore, to practise playing a variety of bunker shots. This will enable you to approach the problem in future with confidence and a knowledge that you can hit the ball onto the green.

Another reason why this shot creates so much anxiety is your perception of what could go wrong when you have to play out of a bunker. Your attitude and behaviour are influenced by past experiences, when you may have taken several shots to get out, or hit the ball so cleanly that it got you into further trouble on the other side of the green.

How well you play future bunker shots will depend upon two things: the first is setting aside time to physically practise correct techniques; the second, and equally important approach, is to counteract negative thinking. For example:

Recognise: Isn't it terrible—my ball's in the bunker and I always seem to have trouble getting out. To make matters worse, the pin is set close to the bunker. I'll have to try and hit the ball gently otherwise I'll never get it close. I hope I don't leave it in the sand.

Challenge: It's not really that bad being there. After all, I know I'm better at these shots than I used to be. I'm glad I practised them this week. I'll just open up the clubface and my stance and keep my weight well forward and take the club back slowly and easily so that I have a slow-motion tempo. I'll let my grip feel a little looser than with other shots and keep my hands a little behind the ball so that I can take a shallow cut of sand.

Respond: But before I start, I'll take a few slow breaths and let my shoulders relax as I settle my feet into the sand. That feels more comfortable. Now, a smooth, slow-motion tempo in my backswing. No need to hurry anything.

Fear of water hazards

If you play on enough golf courses, you will come across a variety of water hazards, including dams, ponds, rivers and even the ocean itself. These are designed to add a degree of difficulty to a hole. While they may be aesthetically interesting, their visual appeal is not the feature that immediately impresses some golfers. Instead, the water hazard is often perceived as an obstacle created to make golf as difficult as possible.

The presence of water, whether to one side of the fairway or as something you have to hit over, seems to immediately engender a sense of fear in many golfers. It is as though it possesses magnetic qualities that will draw your ball into its murky depths. Players will openly admit they are fearful of a water hazard. For example: 'The tee's set well back today. I hope I've got enough club to get over. I always seem to have problems with this drive'.

In this instance, negative self-talk is reinforced by a non-verbal suggestion such as using an old ball. What this action confirms in your mind is that there is every justification for you to think that you are going to lose your ball in the water. As a result of this action, you feel more anxious about the outcome of your shot and your swing becomes inhibited and too fast. Little wonder, then, why you soon come to fear this hazard, especially if it's happened on previous occasions.

Dealing with this frightening hazard is not all that difficult once you realise that you are the one responsible for turning it into an impossible obstacle. The method is the same. Recognise what you are telling yourself, challenge any negative thinking and respond with more positive and appropriate thoughts:

Recognise: If I don't hit it properly, my ball will end up in the water. So I'd better use an old ball.
Challenge: But do I have any definite proof that I'm going to hit it into the water?
Respond: No, I guess I don't, even if I've done it before. If I had nothing else but fairway in front of me, I wouldn't be the slightest bit concerned. So I'm only going to picture the fairway and the point where my ball will land. I'll visualise the ball flying to that point on the fairway and just swing normally.

Using visualisation is preferable to trying not to think of water by pretending it isn't there. As I have explained in Chapter 1, this approach will only reinforce your awareness of the hazard rather than help clear it from your mind.

Picture the fairway as your positive visual focus. The rationale underlying this is that what you see right before you play any shot is what will have the greatest impact on how you hit. In other words, your mind will use this imagery to 'program' your swing so that your shot finishes in the correct position on the fairway.

Putting to save shots

As a golfer, you know how important it is to putt well if you want to score well. Yet putting can cause the greatest problems for some people because it is a stroke which is more susceptible to stress and tension than any other part of the game. It is, after all, a mini-stroke and your judgment of distance and the line of the putt are easily influenced by even the smallest increment of tension in the hands and arms. Self-doubt and negative thinking add to the burden of concentration required and the net result is that your putting stroke disintegrates.

Nothing is more galling for a golfer than to three-putt from five metres after taking the same number of shots over the 500 metres from tee to green. It seems to defy logic unless you realise that putting requires its own individual awareness. You need to have a different mind-set once you reach the green because nothing in the putting stroke bears even a close resemblance to iron and wood shots.

As you crouch over the ball, your anxiety increases and your muscles tense. Your ability to make that short, smooth stroke with the putter has suddenly evaporated. Putting is actually a 'hands and arms' stroke and requires no movement from any other part of your body. Because the margin for error is so small, any superfluous movements are guaranteed to have a major impact on your accuracy and on how you stroke the ball.

How well you putt is often determined by your sense of confidence at that moment. If you have an instinctive feeling you are going to sink a putt, the chances are that it will be successful. But confidence isn't something you can conjure up when you wish. It is a fragile personality trait and is easily undermined. You have only to recall occasions when you have been in the putting doldrums to realise its effects on your game. You anticipate problems long before you reach the green and, when it is your turn to putt, you lose all confidence no matter the distance or the trueness of the green.

Anxiety can become so severe on the green that golfers sometimes develop a condition known as the 'putting yips'. This distressing problem is not uncommon and people who suffer from it virtually 'freeze' over a putt. In some cases the tension and negative thinking are so severe that the golfer is unable to make a backswing with the putter. With others, there is difficulty in following through with the club, resulting in a quick stab at the ball.

All putting problems stem from the amount of tension you feel at that moment. Success depends upon learning how to reduce anxiety and rebuild confidence. Visualisation, correcting negative thinking and relaxation are the cornerstones to beating the putting 'blues'.

Controlled putting

Whenever you are experiencing persistent putting problems, analyse what you are thinking as you walk to a green. You may find that negative thinking starts even while you are still on the fairway:

- Well, I'm on the green. It's not so far from the pin. The way I'm putting these days, there's no guarantee I'll two-putt from there. I don't have any touch at all and the short putts really frighten me.

If this is what you are thinking, challenge its validity:

Challenge: Even if I haven't been putting well lately, does that mean I'm going to continue in this way forever?
Respond: I guess not but it has been going on for a while and nothing I try seems to improve it.
Challenge: But I used to be quite a reasonable putter, so is there

any reason why I can't be a good putter again?

Respond: No, I suppose there isn't but I get so uptight when it's my turn to putt.

Challenge: It's not necessary for me to be tense. After all, it's only a putt and even if I don't get it close to the hole, the world isn't going to come to an end is it?

Respond: No, I guess not. I'll relax over my putt and keep my focus on that point directly behind the ball until it is well on its way to the hole.

Use deep breathing as a relaxation tool while you are waiting to putt or even as you walk to the green. You can reinforce the relaxation process by introducing your cue word, thinking 'CALM' each time you breathe out. A reminder about correct relaxation breathing: Long slow inhalation—pause—long slow exhalation—pause. Make a point of breathing through the nose.

Visualisation techniques are essential if you are to become a sound, consistent putter. When you are standing or crouching behind your ball, picture the line along which you should hit the putt and the correct speed of the ball if it is to reach the hole. You may find it helpful to pick out a blemish or small mark on the line of the putt to focus on. The aim is to narrow your focus of concentration when you are settled over the ball.

As part of visualisation, get a picture fixed in your mind of the ball rolling along the correct line and falling into the cup. You can practise this image over and over while you are waiting your turn to putt. Apart from reinforcing a positive picture, it will also save time and speed up your round.

If you have difficulty 'seeing' your ball following a line to the hole, you may prefer to picture it travelling along a pair of narrow lines similar to a rail track. Many golfers find this easier than trying to visualise a single line pathway. I suggest you experiment with different mental pictures until you find the one that best suits you and then practise using it until it's an established part of your putting routine.

Many professionals maintain you should keep a record of how many putts you take each round. The value of this exercise is that it helps you focus on the importance of each putt. It is worth remembering that, even if you are putting well, the strokes you make on the green can account for almost half your score. The other advantage of keeping a tally of your putts is that it allows you to monitor your progress. However, beware of setting specific goals such as: 'I must take no more than thirty six putts today'. This will only create pressure and you can do without that on the green.

To recap: If putting is a recurrent problem, search for negative thoughts, challenge them, use a relaxation technique and, finally, visualise the line and pace of the putt. Then trust your subconscious—it will prove to be a good friend in the long-term.

CHAPTER SEVEN

Improving Your Scoring

Often your score at the end of a round may not fully reflect how well or poorly you played. It is frustrating when a putt just misses, an approach shot does not hold the green and, even though you are hitting the ball well, your score does not reflect it. However, even if it is not always a true indicator of how well you played, the reality is that your score is the ultimate determinant of success.

A good score happens because you worked for it. It calls for a great deal of mental planning and consideration as well as good form and some luck. In this chapter, I will show you how to deal with two potential problem areas where scoring can be upset. They are:

- Recovering your rhythm.
- Coping with competition.

I also want to show you how to introduce greater consistency in your game. The final element in getting your score to reflect your level of skill is:

- Developing a routine.

Recovering your rhythm

All golfers experience the problem of having a 'bad hole' on occasions and, in the case of most handicap golfers, this generally happens at least once each round. It can occur any time during the game and is always frustrating and demoralising to the player because of uncertainty about why it occurred or when it might occur again. It can strike as early as the first hole or when you are playing well and least expect it.

Unfortunately, when you have a bad hole, it is often the forerunner for a series of bad holes and nothing you do seems to be effective in stopping your slide. The usual response to the problem is to try harder and for most golfers this often involves making dramatic changes to their grip, swing, address or weight distribution. And all this at a time when their mind is already overburdened with anxious thoughts. These sudden changes will only exacerbate the problem and ensure that subsequent holes are fraught with difficulty.

If you are still wondering why a bad hole creates such problems, consider the situation. Here, the difficulty is not in the layout of the course, the prevailing weather conditions or your fellow golfers. It has to come from within yourself and the key triggering factor is anxiety.

We know that it takes very little to start you feeling anxious, and particularly if your life is a stressful one where you feel as if you're 'living on the edge'. Even for a relatively calm person, one poor shot or a single negative thought can be all that is needed to precipitate anxious feelings. This loss of confidence causes you to tighten up and, in a matter of minutes, your swing can be transformed from a silky smooth action to one devoid of any rhythm. Once this happens, your game suddenly falls in a heap and your score climbs.

How do you deal with this recurring nightmare of the bad hole? The most important concern is to get your mind back on track as soon as possible but this is not easy unless you are equipped with the right techniques. There are two principal targets to aim at: anxiety and negative self-talk. These are closely linked but it's easier to deal with them separately when you are on the course. Here is a modification of the challenge exercise that might be helpful:

1. The first step you must take after having a 'bad hole' is to analyse the negative things you are saying to yourself at that moment. You can be sure there will be a host of these present:
   - I made a mess of that hole. I should have parred and, instead, I had a double bogey. I hope the rest of my game isn't going to be like that.

2. Step two involves quickly using positive thoughts to redirect yourself to positive actions:
   - Obviously, I feel a bit tense and upset about that. If I continue to worry about it, it'll affect the rest of my game. That hole is finished now and nothing I do can change the score.

I'm just going to relax and focus only on the next shot. That's the only thing I have control over at this moment.

3. Reinforce step 2 by using controlled breathing to relax:
   - As I wait my turn to hit, I'll use the time to relax. I'll slow everything down by concentrating on my breathing. Long, slow in-breaths and long, slow out-breaths. I'll keep this going until I set-up for the tee shot. No need to rush or hurry anything.

4. Continue this positive approach by reinforcing confidence in your swing:
   - My tension probably caused a lot of the problems on the last hole but there's no reason why I should try and change anything in my game at the moment. I'll leave everything as it is and let my normal swing take over rather than tinker with things.

5. When you have made that successful hit and feel your rhythm has returned, reinforce this with more positive thoughts:
   - Now, that shot felt a lot better. I'm going to walk slowly and steadily to my ball and continue my slow breathing as I do. I know I can enjoy the rest of my game and still put in a good card.

This successful sequence should be enough to restore your equanimity and give you the confidence that you can overcome a missed shot or a bad hole whenever it happens.

Coping with competition

Have you ever considered why you are able to hit perfect shots during a practice round or on the practice fairway and yet be unable to repeat these during competition? The reason is the pressure created by the desire to succeed. In other words, you become anxious about the outcome of shots instead of trusting your swing and hitting the ball in a relaxed, focused manner. A fear or expectation of failure overcomes you and your confidence is undermined by negative self-talk.

One of the most common results of this anxiety is the urge to hit the ball as hard as possible. It may be stimulated by the conscious or unconscious desire to match others' shots, or by the sheer length of a hole. Weather, too, can play its part, especially the presence of wind. Many golfers find that whenever they have to hit into a substantial breeze, some sort of gremlin takes over in their mind that causes them to swing faster in the mistaken belief they need to hit the ball harder than usual.

You may have noticed that when this uncontrollable desire to hit the ball as hard as possible takes over, it rarely meets with success. Forcing your swing usually causes you to stray into unchartered rough and this will always undermine your score in competition. The most curious feature of this behaviour is that even though you may consciously acknowledge that trying to hit the ball too hard is unrewarding, it is seemingly impossible to resist.

Changing your mental attitude to competition is the practical way to succeed. You must remind yourself that you are playing against yourself rather than against other golfers. Once you counteract the belief that you have to match others and, instead, simply play within yourself, you remove a great many pressures from your game. As professional David Graham points out:

> 'Golf is a game you play against yourself. There is no one to blame for your failures except you. The credit for your successes goes to you alone ... The more you put into it, the more you get out of it'.

Here are a few basic ground rules which will help you develop a better psychological approach to competition.

Playing to your handicap

Mentally play each hole to your handicap rather than believe that you must make par. Remember that each hole has been rated by its degree of difficulty and although par may be a possibility for you to achieve, it should not be the primary goal. If, for example, you have a handicap of 18 or above, play each hole in your mind as if bogey is your par. In other words, a par four becomes a par five and so on. The reason for adopting this approach is that you remove an element of pressure from your game. As a result, the chances are that you will swing with more confidence and often this leads to your shooting par on that hole in any case. When this happens, view it as a pleasant and unexpected bonus and congratulate yourself.

Playing in the present

One advantage of playing a practice round is that most golfers remain focused on the 'here-and-now' shot rather than allowing themselves to be distracted by previous or future possibilities.

This situation tends to change in competition and you may find yourself caught up in thinking about a previous bad shot or hole, or planning how you are going to play the next few holes.

Interestingly, this can even happen when you're playing well and realise that you may be able to beat your handicap or even win the competition. In that situation, your mind is besieged by thoughts such as:

- If I shoot no worse than one-over for the last three holes, I could win this.

Have you any idea of what sort of pressures that negative thinking creates? In no time at all, you tighten up, your swing quickens and what could have been a good round turns out to be no more than an illusion.

To deal with this problem, try altering your game plan. Instead of playing the round as eighteen holes or two sets of nine, follow 'The Rule of Three' or 'The Rule of Six'. Evaluate how you are performing after each set of three or six holes. No matter how well or poorly you have played one set, approach the next set with an entirely fresh attitude. In other words, mentally close the door on previous scores and focus only on the immediate shot. As with all these techniques, you will need to practise to gain the maximum benefits but it is worthwhile and may surprise you when you tally up your card at the end of the round.

Playing to imperfection

Accept the fact that it is rare for most handicap golfers to hit every shot with precision and there is every chance that you will end up in the rough at some point. Sometimes, you will find your ball in situations where it is just not possible to play a shot in the direction of the green. Nevertheless, many golfers become obsessed with trying to rectify the problem by hitting an impossible recovery shot. For example, they may attempt to fire the ball through a gap in the trees which would intimidate even the most skilled professional. The rule is be sensible and cautious, and acknowledge that in the majority of cases, this approach will fail and only complicate an already difficult situation.

Accept that you have to sacrifice a shot and pursue the only intelligent course of action: 'The Rule of Conservatism'. Even if this means playing the ball sideways or backwards, it is a shot which requires a great deal of thought and consideration and should never be rushed. Your aim is to put the ball in a position from which you can recover lost ground.

Unfortunately, what often happens is that a golfer is so stressed by this situation that all semblance of clear thinking and focus is forgotten, and the result is an inappropriate shot. Usually, this will cost you at least one extra stroke and you will probably still find yourself in an impossible situation for your next shot. Before this occurs, try to slow everything down. Breathe easily, use a relaxation cue and then plan the shot that will put you in the best position to recover.

Playing your established game

During competition, don't make major adjustments to your game or swing no matter what happens on the course. Obviously, it is commonsense to make appropriate allowances, for example if you have a tendency to fade or draw shots on a particular day.

However, any major changes in swing pattern or grip break down the unconscious mental circuits you have carefully built up in your brain, causing it to send the wrong messages to your muscles. This will only complicate your problems.

If your swing lacks its normal fluid feel and you are playing below your usual form, accept the situation and decide that any major problems should be sorted out on the practice tee. Unfortunately, many golfers make competition far too arduous for themselves by clinging to the erroneous belief that they should be able to play to their maximum potential each time they go to the course. This is simply not possible, for we all have imperfections and shortcomings in the way we play the game just as we do in everyday life. If you remember to use 'The Rule of Acceptance' and realise that some rounds are going to be less than desirable, you will achieve a great deal more satisfaction and enjoyment from your game.

Playing the day of competition

On the day of the match, do everything as though you are operating at half-speed. Even such things as having a shower, getting dressed and driving to the club should be done in a leisurely fashion. Your aim is to establish a sense of tempo in your movements which will carry through to your golf, so avoid rushing, especially before a competition round.

Go through your pre-game and first tee techniques which help you to relax and let go of tensions and self-imposed limitations. Follow the same pre-shot routine each time you hit, including using your breathing to relax your arms, hands, shoulders and legs.

If you mishit the ball, acknowledge this as being imperfect but, rather than get upset about it, use it as a stimulus to relax and focus more closely on the next shot. Reassure yourself, too, that one poor hit doesn't mean you will repeat it and that you can play the rest of your shots with ease.

Developing a routine

Like most sports, golf requires you to develop a routine if you want to play to your maximum ability and enjoy the game. But what is a golf routine and why is it so important? A routine is simply the process of going through a repetitious pattern of exercises so that you are reminded to do things that are beneficial to some aspect of your game. A good example of this is the set-up routine you diligently follow before hitting the ball. You may have noticed that your swing is not comfortable unless you go through the pre-shot sequence in a fixed order. Establishing a routine is no more than developing a habit and sticking to it.

A golf routine is not only used during a round. It is also useful to establish routines for preparation at home, on the practice range and during competition that will improve your performance. The aim is to develop a set of habits which will help you relax, pace yourself and play to your potential.

Home routines

Have you ever considered how often you think about some aspect of golf when you are at home or in a situation far removed from the course? The chances are that some notion about the game enters your mind more frequently than you realise and this usually indicates how important the sport is in your life. If you are serious about your golf, why not replace these unstructured thinking times with techniques that will improve your approach?

The following routines can be part of a home training regime:

- Set aside time each day to practise the Creative Relaxation exercises described in Chapter 8. They are essential if you are a person who tends to get excessively anxious or tense in competition. The techniques also help you 'reprogram' your mind and improve your golf through the use of affirmations and visualisation.
- If you are unable or simply can't spend time using relaxation techniques, you can practise another form of mental rehearsal. Sit quietly in a chair with your eyes closed and, for at least five minutes, picture a golf scene in your mind's eye. It may be associated with your swing, putting or playing a few holes in an ideal way.
- Apart from mental preparation, it is important to establish a routine when preparing your golfing accoutrements. As Killara Golf Club pro David Mercer says: 'If your shoes and clubs are clean at the start of a game, it helps you feel more confident and shows others that you feel good about yourself'.

Practice routines

Using routines during practice sessions is necessary if you are serious about improving your game. Why else do professionals and low handicap players spend hours on the practice fairway and putting green? Practice gives you the opportunity to establish habits, as well as helping you work on your technique. However, to achieve the full benefit from practice, you should use the time to establish your routine. It is easier to do this in practice than when you are playing under the pressure of competition.

Here are some routines that can be used on the practice tee:

- Before your practice session, spend a few moments taking a series of long, slow inhalations and exhalations through your nose. It may seem curious to you, at this point, that you should practise something as natural as breathing. However, few people know how to breathe correctly or how to use it for relaxation purposes. The aim in all the exercises is to have them so ingrained that you use them automatically when you are under pressure.

- Spend a few minutes standing with your feet together and swing the club backwards and forwards. Develop a rhythm in your swing by timing the backswing to coincide with your in-breath and the forward swing with your out-breath.

- Go through your pre-shot routine of focusing on the grip, alignment, ball position in your stance and visualisation of the shot you're going to hit. With visualisation, imagine that you are playing to a particular green rather than some distant point on a fairway. You can intensify this process by playing a game within yourself and imagining that it is this final shot that will decide the outcome of a match or a competition.

- If you are practising chip shots around the green, never deviate from the set routine you use with tee shots. In this case though, you may need to spend a little longer on the visualisation process, 'seeing' the clubhead making contact with the ball, its trajectory before landing on the green and any 'run' it may have.

- On the green, practise relaxation breathing and visualising the line that your putt should follow before dropping into the hole.

Pre-game routines

We know that many golfers rush to the course and on to the first tee without having carried out any preparatory exercises. While this is not a recommended way of approaching a round, if you have ever been in this situation, you probably found it difficult to pace yourself and tended to rush your shots, walked quickly and generally played well below your best form until you 'settled down'.

You have started your game still under the influence of outside pressures, a common cause for massive adrenaline release. Since it is not possible to suddenly switch off this reaction, it will affect the way you play. If you can restructure the free time available before a game, even the shortest pre-game routine can help you establish the rhythm you need at the start. Shortcut routines for people 'on the go' include:

- Use controlled breathing for the few minutes you are sitting quietly in your parked car. As a reminder: long slow in-breath—pause—long slow out-breath—pause.
- As you walk to the first tee, breathe easily and slowly through the nose.
- Use visualisation to picture the shot you are going to play from the first tee.

- Waiting your turn to hit can be a productive time. Keep your mind occupied by visualising the shot you are going to play on this hole.
- Another routine you can use on the first tee is to alternately tense and relax your hands. Reminder: Each time you breathe in, tighten the hands into a fist; as you breathe out, relax the hands, arms and shoulders. When this is performed slowly, it can be an effective and rapid way of relieving tension.

Although these routines require 10 to 20 minutes of free time before a game, the reward will far outweigh the extra effort involved.

Competition routines

During a competition round there are several good routines that will improve your game plan. Each player should decide which aspect of their game needs emphasis and choose a routine that works for them:

- Use a pre-shot routine to focus on grip, alignment, ball position and visualisation of the shot.
- Remember to change your mental camera lens to a wide-angle one after you have played the shot.
- Always walk to your ball steadily and without rushing no matter where the previous shot finished.
- As you set up for the next hit, switch to your close-up lens before your pre-shot routine. Use the cue of the ball itself or

taking your club from the bag as a reminder to change to your narrow focus.

- The closer your approach is to the green, the more time you should spend on visualising.
- When you are putting, switch to your close-up lens to maintain a narrow focus of concentration from the moment you address the ball until it is in the hole.
- Picture the correct line and pace of the putt so that you are able to make the right judgment about the stroke required.

Final score

There are no magic tricks to improving scoring but the ideas we have discussed will be effective in reducing your anxiety about your final score. While it is not possible, at first, for you to incorporate all of these techniques into your game, be patient. I suggest that you select one or two procedures and practise these until they are a permanent part of your game. Then expand your repertoire as you need to.

Initially, it is worthwhile getting an overview of the techniques by reading through the whole series, mainly because one procedure tends to link into another. This overlap is to be expected for it is impossible to 'pigeon-hole' the mind into rigid compartments. However, even though there is a certain amount of continuity between techniques, each golf situation requires a slightly different approach.

How you deal with the pressure of competition and scoring will depend on how diligently you practise, both physically and mentally. Remember that changing behaviour takes time as well as practice, so don't expect a sudden surge of success. Bad habits become fixed through repetition and it takes time and effort to undo them and replace them with more desirable ones. These unwanted behaviours may still surface occasionally but now you will know how to counteract them.

CHAPTER EIGHT

Creative Relaxation

The ultimate goal most golfers would like to achieve is the ability to play every round in the 'Zone'. But, what is this 'Zone' we all crave to attain? It is not easy to give you a precise definition mainly because it incorporates many different experiences. Tour professional David Graham describes the 'Zone' as 'a magical state of mind . . . where everything takes on a dreamy, tranquil quality and you are in complete control of your mind and body'. He also likens it to being in a hypnotic state.

Playing in the 'Zone'

The hallmark of playing in the 'Zone' is that every part of your game seems effortless and free from strain. It is as though you are expending no excess mental energy. You feel relaxed but focused and your mind is completely free of intrusive, bothersome thoughts. There is an underlying sense of confidence in the way you play your shots and your swing is relaxed, rhythmical and effortless. As a result, you hit the ball with a perfect swing and expect every shot to be successful. You feel that you are playing within yourself no matter what happens during the game.

The chances are that you may have had this experience on more than one occasion and played outstanding golf. The problem is that it is a transient state and is impossible to capture through conscious willpower. Somehow, the harder you try to experience it, the less likely it will happen.

Playing in the 'Zone' means you have a sense of ease and naturalness throughout your game. It would seem reasonable to expect that if you could always be relaxed on the course, this should guarantee achieving this 'magical state' more often. Unfortunately, it is not that easy, and the usual stumbling block is anxiety.

We've shown that anxiety is a common enough experience and can have a profound influence on your golf. As a tour professional, David Graham has noted its damaging effects: 'Golfers rarely play to their handicap in competition because of their inability to lower their anxiety level. Anxiety is destructive, and it doesn't take much to let it creep into your psyche'.

Walking the mental plank

Competition rounds are a source of anxiety for most golfers. Many people are able to play a practice round without difficulty and even achieve pars with monotonous regularity but are unable to repeat their performance when they are confronted by a weekend match. The most obvious reason for this is that they have let the pressure of competition override all their carefully practised golfing techniques.

I term this phenomenon 'walking the mental plank' and it happens in all sports. Let me explain what I mean. If I asked you to walk along a 30 cm wide plank laid out on the ground, I'm sure you would have no difficulty in complying. But if I suspended that same plank about 30 metres off the ground and asked you to walk on it, the chances are that you would hesitate, perhaps take tentative, abnormally slow steps or you would simply refuse to do it.

It is exactly the same plank but because in the second case, anxiety, fear and an element of danger entered the picture, it changed your whole perspective of the situation.

The same situation can occur in golf. Competition adds elements of unpredictability, pressure and, perhaps, fear. This is why it is valuable to learn ways that will reduce your chances of becoming anxious. While no one can anticipate when they might feel anxious during a round, if you have developed and used relaxation techniques, you reduce the odds of being overly affected.

Relaxation exercises allow you greater control over the unconscious part of your reactions. Even though inherited skills, coaching and practice play a major role, the mind determines if you are ultimately successful. Professional Jenny Sevil sums up the vital role the mind plays:

> 'Most professionals are of a fairly equivalent standard when it comes to skills. In the long-term, the thing which makes the difference between success and failure is how well you control your mind. I believe that the mind's contribution can be anything up to 80% of the game'.

Using Creative Relaxation

There are many techniques available which will help you relax. If you already use meditation, yoga or a relaxation exercise you feel comfortable with, I suggest you continue to use it.

The Creative Relaxation process I recommend has some distinct advantages over other techniques. Based on the self-hypnotic approach, it enables you to 'reprogram' your mind by linking suggestions and imagery with an intense state of relaxation. This ability to 'work' on your own mind and gradually correct those things that interfere with your golf, gives you much greater control on the course. If you find it difficult to relax without someone else's voice guiding the process, a relaxation audio tape can be helpful until you are able to do the exercises on your own. The accompanying audio CD is a good starting point in helping you relax.

When and where to relax

Let us start by considering how you achieve a relaxed state. Selecting a suitable time and place to practise is important. Most of us lead busy lives and, for this reason, it is not always possible to make time for relaxation. Try to choose a time of the day when you are not under pressure or obligated to rush off and do other things.

I suggest that the morning is the best time for practice since your mind is still fresh and you will find it easier to concentrate. I would even suggest that if you are serious about improving your approach to golf, it would be worthwhile setting your alarm 15 minutes earlier. This may appear to be robbing you of precious sleep time but usually your plane of sleep before waking is so shallow that you won't miss out on the beneficial effects by getting up 15 minutes early.

From the point of view of refreshing your mind, the time spent on achieving deep relaxation is probably equivalent to many hours sound sleep and has the added benefit of making you feel good for the rest of the day. On the other hand, doing these exercises too late in the day will be difficult because your mind is tired and you will probably find yourself drifting off to sleep as you become relaxed.

For the same reason, it is not a good idea to do these mental exercises while in bed. Over the years, you have built up a strong relationship between bed and sleep so it will be difficult to resist going to sleep as you become relaxed. Relaxation is different from sleep, being a focused, active state rather than passive and unconscious. So, select a comfortable chair with a back high enough to support your head. You can also lie on the floor on a blanket or sponge rubber camping mat and use a cushion for your head if this is more comfortable.

Loosen any tight clothing. If it is cold make sure you are warmly dressed or have a heater on in the room. Relaxation will slow down your body's metabolism and unless you take these precautions, you can easily become chilled. Not only will you find this uncomfortable but it will act as a distraction and interfere with your ability to keep your mind focused.

People often ask me how much time they should spend on relaxation techniques and how often they should do them? You will find that achieving a relaxed state, instilling positive thoughts and using imagery will take about 20 minutes of concentrated effort.

Daily practice of these mental exercises is the most effective way of producing change. However, if your routine makes it difficult for you to use these techniques every day, do them as often as you can. Remember, though, the more you use them the more your game will improve.

The process of achieving mental fitness is similar to becoming physically fit and yet few people see it that way. If you want to get physically fit you have to be prepared to exercise on a regular basis. Good mental fitness calls for the same sort of dedication.

When you first start using relaxation exercises, set aside 'special time' for your routine. Make a commitment to yourself that you will do this for at least three weeks in the beginning. By the end of that period you will notice many beneficial effects and you will have developed a habit that soon becomes an established part of your daily routine.

Achieving Creative Relaxation

The techniques I am about to describe to you are ones that have benefited thousands of my patients over the years. They have the advantage of being easy to understand and practise and lead to a deep sense of mental and physical relaxation. If you are not familiar with relaxation techniques, a number of things may unsettle you at first. You may feel restless and fidgety or have difficulty keeping your mind focused on each procedure because of the stray thoughts that interrupt your concentration. These are problems that everyone experiences and will become less troublesome with practice.

The other thing I should mention is the need to 'let things happen rather than 'trying to make them happen'. This is not an easy concept to accept, because, from early childhood, we have been indoctrinated with the need for conscious striving if we are to succeed. However, relaxation is one exception to this rule and 'trying to relax' will only make you more tense. So, settle back in your chair and guide yourself slowly and effortlessly through each part of the relaxation process. Your aim is to avoid consciously scrutinising your inner experiences. Instead, just let things happen.

There are four procedures I recommend. Each of these has a special role and each has a cumulative effect on the others; the final goal being a calm, relaxed mind and body. First, you will go through a process of slowing your breathing. Next, you will learn how to physically relax your body. This will be followed by the stilling and quietening of the mind. Finally, you will use a technique that is designed to deepen your overall state of relaxation. Although all these procedures play a part, the most important is the quietening of your mind. You will probably find it is the hardest to apply but don't be discouraged. It will get better with practice.

Developing rhythmical breathing

Settle yourself in your chair or in your chosen position for relaxation and begin the process by closing your eyes. In the first few minutes focus on breathing and try to achieve long, slow, unforced inhalations, followed by a short pause of relaxed emptiness until your need to breathe out prompts a passive exhalation.

Although breathing is an unconscious act, it is always surprising how few people know how to do it correctly. As I have emphasised, it is important to establish a rhythmical pattern in which you breathe in and out through the nose. This will take getting used to if you are in the habit of being a mouth breather. While slowly breathing in, get the feeling that each inhalation is pushing your waist out sideways. This is diaphragmatic breathing. It is essential for good relaxation and for opening-up the lower air passages of your lungs so that with each breath, you are able to take in far more oxygen.

Establishing a relaxed breathing rhythm is a valuable way of reducing tensions. You will notice that your long, slow exhalations are accompanied by sensations of sinking, widening, softening and feelings of comfort, heaviness and warmth. The effect is an overall mood of patience and calmness.

Relaxing your body

Once you have established a slow, regular breathing rhythm, it is time to relax your body. I will describe the technique in the first person so that you can learn the correct way of using it. The suggestions for relaxation are recited slowly and silently so that they coincide with the exhalation part of the breathing cycle. I have inserted '. . .' to show you where to use the inhalation phase as a pause between suggestions:

- As I focus on the muscles of my face . . . each time I breathe out . . . I feel as though I'm breathing away all the tension . . . My eyelids become so heavy . . . heavier and heavier . . . they feel like lead shutters . . . my jaw muscles are so relaxed . . . my lips part quite naturally . . . my face feels soft . . . soft and relaxed.

- That ease is flowing into my scalp ... into my neck ... my head is so heavy against the back of the chair.
- It flows into my shoulders ... as I breathe out ... I am breathing away all the tension ... all the strain from my shoulder muscles ... letting-go of it completely.
- I can feel the ease flowing into my upper arms ... into my forearms ... wrists ... hands ... it's as though I'm gently pushing all the tension ... all the strain ... out through my fingertips.
- The ease flows into my upper back ... my chest ... like a gentle sensation of warmth ... it flows into my lower back ... my tummy ... my whole body feels so comfortable ... so heavy.
- As I breathe out slowly ... I feel the ease in my hips ... thighs ... in my lower legs ... ankles ... feet ... I am letting-go of the tension feelings through my toes ... as I breathe out each time.

Quietening your mind

The body relaxation process will take several minutes. Once you feel your body is relaxed, it is time to relax your mind. The aim of the following procedure is to allow your mind to be as still, focused and centred as possible. In order to do this, think of the word 'CALM' as you slowly exhale. You should use this word as you would a mantra in meditation.

'CALM' has connotations of peace and tranquillity for most people. You may notice that other thoughts keep intruding.

Unfortunately, this can happen and it is best to treat them as if they are quite incidental. Feel as though these thoughts are flowing in through one ear and out through the other and draw your mind back to 'CALM' as you breathe out slowly. After a while, disturbing thoughts will fade into the background and no longer trouble you.

Sometimes you may find it impossible to keep your mind focused for any length of time on 'CALM' without being distracted. This is more likely to occur when you are feeling overly stressed. If this happens, you can use a modification of the focusing technique.

As you breathe in, begin counting so that with the first in-breath you count 'ONE' to yourself and as you breathe out, you think 'CALM'. Then, with the next in-breath you count 'TWO' and again think 'CALM' as you exhale. Keep doing this until you reach 'FOUR' and then return to 'ONE' and start again. The aim is to help keep your mind occupied and focused so that it is always involved in the relaxation process.

It may take some time to empty your mind of bothersome thoughts. However, with practice it becomes easier to quieten your mind and achieve a much greater sense of detachment or disengagement from your everyday world. Once you have had this first beautiful experience, you will become aware of how cluttered and anxious your mind has been in the past. It may take time to reach this stage but it is worth the effort.

People often ask how long should the mental focusing session take? There are no fixed rules but I usually recommend that you focus on the word 'CALM' until your mind is relatively quiet. You won't achieve complete stillness at first, so be satisfied with a reduction in your 'mental noise' or 'mental static'.

Deepening your relaxation

By the time you have reached this point of relaxation, you may feel that it is impossible to go any deeper. However, you can experience an even deeper state of mental and physical ease. There are a variety of ways of doing this but one of the simplest and most effective is through counting.

Again, pace your counting to coincide with each slow exhalation. Some people like to visualise themselves walking down steps to a peaceful scene, while others imagine walking along stepping stones that take them over a small stream. If you prefer to use visualisation or anything that will enhance your sense of involvement, do so. Remember, '. . .' have been inserted to show you where to use an inhalation as a pause between suggestions:

- Now that I'm relaxed . . . I feel as though I would like to go even deeper . . . as I count silently I'll let each number carry me even further into relaxation.
- ONE . . . becoming more and more relaxed.
- TWO . . .
- THREE . . . more and more at peace.
- FOUR . . .
- FIVE . . .
- SIX . . . deeper and deeper relaxed.
- SEVEN . . .
- EIGHT . . . so much more at peace.

- NINE . . .
- TEN . . . completely relaxed all through me.

By this stage, you will feel complete mental and physical relaxation. This is a wonderful sensation but you must use this state of mind so that it works to your advantage the next time you play golf. You have dug the mental garden, so to speak. What you decide to plant in it will determine whether you have undesirable weeds (a stressful, poor game) or beautiful flowers (a relaxed, satisfying round).

Using affirmations

Creative Relaxation is a state where your mind feels slightly detached from things around you. You are aware that these things are there but they don't intrude. It is also a state in which the mind is extremely sensitive to any suggestions or mental imagery you give yourself. This is what makes this technique so valuable.

The thoughts you silently present to yourself may be associated with success in golf or other things you want to achieve in life. Keep these suggestions as simple as possible. You can usually instil a number of positive thoughts each session. Typical examples would be:

- As I relax more each day, I feel more at ease in every aspect of my game.
- My whole swing feels comfortable and relaxed and I can hit the ball with a sense of timing and rhythm.
- My head is still when I hit the ball.

- I can put each hole I've played behind me and focus only on the present shot.

You will note that I've expressed these positive thoughts in the present tense which ensures that you think of the messages as something that can happen now rather than in the future. These suggestions are also specific, which is a deliberate attempt to direct your thinking towards a positive outcome on the golf course.

Visualisation in the relaxed state

Creative Relaxation provides an ideal opportunity for using visualisation. Your mind is still, untroubled by extraneous thoughts and you can focus more intensely on pictures and events. You will find that you can imagine situations with far greater clarity than at other times and this feature is an advantage when you want to use the technique for mental rehearsal.

Picture some aspect of your game you want to improve. It may be something to do with your swing or the way you play a particular hole. Visualise it in as much detail as you can, 'seeing', for example, the colour of the grass, the logo on the ball or the clubface being lined up behind the ball in your set-up. You can then move on to aspects that you want to correct but be sure to let the pictures develop without too much conscious effort on your part.

While visualisation is a relaxing and involving process, its effects are far-reaching. You will notice changes in your game as soon as these exercises have become a regular part of your practice regime. Relaxation will be a natural and effortless part of your game. This is because you have done the necessary preparation and practice to ensure your success.

Good golf

The value of the techniques described in this book and their success in using the mind more effectively on the golf course are supported by a wealth of research and anecdotal data. The three key elements in playing better golf are:

- **centre** on relaxation
- **focus** your concentration correctly
- **fine-tune** your visualisation skills

If you incorporate these techniques into your game each time you play, you can be sure that they will bring you success and make each round of golf a far more enjoyable experience.

References

Baker-Finch, Ian, Australian tour professional, 1991 British Open champion, Personal communication.

Graham, David (1990) *Mental Toughness Training for Golf*, Ringwood, Victoria, Penguin Books.

Hohnen, Greg, Professional, The Killara Golf Club, Sydney, Personal communication.

Jackson, Arthur (1989), *Stress Control Through Self-Hypnosis*, Sydney, Doubleday.

Jackson, Arthur (1992), *Achieving Calm Through Creative Relaxation*, No. 4, Creative Relaxation audio tape series.

Jencks, Beata, (1978), 'Utilising the phases of the breathing rhythm in hypnosis', F.H. Frankel & H.S. Zamansky (Eds), *Hypnosis at its Bicentennial*, New York, Plenum Press.

Mercer, David, Senior professional, The Killara Golf Club, Sydney, Personal communication.

Nicklaus, Jack (1976), *Golf my Way*, London, Pan Books Ltd.

Norman, Greg, Video: *Greg Norman's Golf Clinic*, Narrabeen, NSW, Celebrity Sports International Pty Ltd.

Rules of Golf (1992), The Royal and Ancient Golf Club of St. Andrews.

Sevil, Jennifer, Australian tour professional on the Australian and Japanese circuits, Australian Woman Golfer of the Year, 1992, Highest money-earning Australian sportswoman, 1992, Personal communication.

Index

adrenaline rushes 3–4, 37, 66, 67, 68, 100
affirmations 24, 28, 115–16
alignment 56–7, 61
anxiety
  adrenaline rushes and 4, 37
  bunkers and 80–1
  competition and 105, 106
  concentration and 5, 6, 9
  first tee 74–9
  inner voice and 12
  intrusion of 2–3, 14, 105
  negative thinking and 14, 15, 16, 27, 32, 67
  pace and 66–8
  pre-game 52–3
  putting and 84–5
  rhythm and 89–90
  tension and 3, 4, 63, 84, 85
approach shots 28–31
audio tapes, relaxation 107
awareness, mental 49–50

Baker-Finch, Ian 45
blood sugar reserves 4
breathing
  chest 53
  controlled 52–3, 69, 75–6, 91, 96, 100
  creative relaxation and 110–11
  deep 68, 86
  diaphragmatic 52, 111
  nasal 52–3, 55–6, 65, 68
  pre-game anxiety and 52–3, 100, 101
  relaxation cues and 65–6, 75
  rhythmical 53, 110–11
bunkers 80–1

CALM cue 53, 65, 68, 72, 86 112–13
camera lenses, mental 7–10, 45, 59, 60, 61–2, 72, 101
challenge exercise 22–37, 64
challenging 22, 24, 26–7, 29–30, 32–4, 35–6, 37, 81, 82, 83, 85–6
chip shots 99–100
close-up lenses 8–9, 10, 60, 61, 62, 101

coaching 12,49
cognitive restructuring *see* challenge exercise
competition
anxiety and 92, 105, 106
coping with 92–7
routines for 101–2
concentration
adrenaline and 4
changing your 60–3
difficulties with 5–6
first tee anxiety and 74, 77–8
focus and 7, 8–10, 45, 60–3, 72
narrowing of 77–8
overloading and 5
putting and 84, 102
confidence
bunkers and 80
competition and 92
putting and 84, 85
rhythm and 90
sell-belief and 13–16, 21
conscious effort 6, 11, 12
counting 113, 114–15
Creative Relaxation 98, 104–17
cues 62–3, 65–6, 72, 86, 95

dams 82
distractions 70–1, 77–8, 100
see also intrusive thinking
expectations 5, 92

family pressures 5
fear
bunker shots and 80
competition and 106
illogical nature of 18, 23
water hazards and 82
final score 102–3
first tee 25–8, 72, 74–9, 96
fist clenches 75, 101
focus 7–10, 59, 60, 61, 101, 102

game plans 94
goals 16
Graham, David 41, 42, 93, 104, 105
grip
tension in 36, 54, 67
visualisation of 56

handicap, playing to 93
hazards *see* bunkers; water hazards
Hohnen, Greg 45–6, 55
home routines 97–8
humour 27, 30

intrusive thinking 5, 31–4
see also distractions
intuition *see* subconscious mind
lenses, mental camera 7–10, 45, 59, 60, 61–2, 72, 101

Locke, Bobby ix
looking-up 37
loosening-up 75–6
see also warm-ups

memory cues 61–3
mental camera lenses 7–10, 45, 59, 60, 61–2, 72, 101

mental pictures *see* visualisation
mental rehearsal 47–50, 55, 58–60, 98, 116–117 *see also* relaxation
mental relaxation 112–13 *see also* CALM cue
Mercer, David 41–2, 46, 98
moods 69
muscle tension 3, 4, 36–7, 84, 85

negative self-talk phrases 18, 23
negative thinking/self-talk
  anxiety and 2–3, 5, 6, 9, 14, 15, 16, 27, 33, 67
  background to 17–21
  bunkers and 81
  challenging of 22, 24, 26–7, 29–30, 32–5
  competition and 92, 94
  concentration and 5–6, 9
  confidence and 14, 15
  first tee anxiety and 74, 76–7
  overcoming 20–1
  phrases used in 18, 23
  putting and 84, 85–6
  recognising 22, 23, 25–6, 29, 31–2, 37, 81, 82, 83
  rhythm and 90
  water hazards and 82–3
  see also anxiety; tension
Newton, Jack ix–x
Nicklaus, Jack x, 36, 40–1, 42, 74, 79
Norman, Greg 36, 40

overload xiv–xv, 5, 14

pacing 66–9
people problems 70–1
personal issues 5, 31–4, 69, 71
personality 69–70
phrases
  recognising negative self-talk 18, 23
    stock challenge exercise 35
picture imagery *see* visualisation
Player, Gary 47
ponds 82
positive thinking/self-talk
  affect on game of 16–17
  affirmations and 115–16
  examples of 78
  first tee anxiety and 78
  relaxation problems and 71–2
  replacing tension with 64–5
  responding with 22, 24, 28, 30–1, 34, 36, 78, 83, 86, 90–1
practice
  mental 45–50, 55, 58–60, 98, 99–100
  physical 50, 54, 81, 93, 99
  pre-game 54, 55, 72, 96, 97, 99–100
practice routines 98–100
pre-game routines 100–1
pressure, mental 5, 31, 92, 94, 100, 105, 106
problem holes
  rehearsal of 48–9
  see also bunkers; first tee; water hazards

problem solving course guide
 73–87
professionals and visualisation
 39–43
putting 39, 44, 83–7, 102

radio station, inner 44
rehearsal, mental 47–50, 55,
 58–60, 98, 99–100
relaxation
 competition and 92–3
 deepening your 114–15
 mental 112–13
 physical 111–12
 problems with 71–2
 putting and 85
 rhythmical breathing for 110–11
 technique for 72, 75–6, 86, 98,
 107–17
 visualisation and 41, 116–17
 when and where of 107–9
 see also affirmations; Creative
 Relaxation
relaxation audio tapes 107
relaxation cues 62–3, 65–6, 72, 86,
 95
RELEASE cue 75
responding 22, 24, 28, 30–1, 34, 37,
 82, 83, 85, 86
rhythm 15, 37, 55, 89–91, 99, 100
rivers 82
routines 97–102

scoring improvement 88–103
seeing your game 45–7
self-belief 13–16
self-doubt 2, 14, 15, 17, 84
self-talk *see* negative thinking/self-talk;
 positive thinking/self-talk
set-up routine
 concentration during 7
 four-step sequence for 41–2
Sevil, Jenny 16, 19-20, 44, 106
subconscious mind 4, 6, 10–12, 30,
 31, 39, 50, 57
swing
 adrenaline surges and 4
 coaching for 12
 competition and 95, 96
 forcing of 92
 inconsistence of 2–3, 11–12
 muscle tension and 4, 36, 37
 negative thinking and 14, 15, 16
 practice of 12, 49–50
 rehearsal of 49–50, 59
 rhythm and 55
 visualisation of 49–50, 59

tempo 15, 16, 37, 96
tension
 anxiety and 3, 4, 63, 69, 84, 85
 controlled breathing and 75, 111
 negative thoughts and 3, 14, 16,
 36–7
 on-course 63–6
 positive thinking and 64–5, 91
 putting and 84, 85
 recognition of 63–4
 relaxation and 65, 72, 111
 see also grip

thoughts 16–17
  see also intrusive thinking; negative thinking/self-talk; positive thinking/self-talk
Trevino, Lee 7

visualisation
  competition and 101, 102
  first tee anxiety and 74, 78–9, 100–1
  how to use 43–50
  introduction to 38–9
  practice routines and 55–6, 99–100
  professionals use of 39–43
  putting and 85, 86–7
  relaxation and 72, 114, 116–17
  sharpening skills of 55–66
  water hazards and 83

WII FM 44
warm-ups 54, 55
  see also loosening-up
water hazards 82–3
what-ifs 2–3, 18
wide-angle lenses 8, 9, 10, 59, 60, 61, 101
willpower 6, 12, 67, 105
wind 92
worry 33–4

yips, putting 84–5

'Zone', playing in the 104–5